Women at the Crossroads

Women at the Crossroads

A Prostitute Community's Response to AIDS in Urban Senegal

Michelle Lewis Renaud

Routledge
New York and London

Published in 1997 by
Routledge
Taylor & Francis Group
270 Madison Avenue
New York, NY 10016

Published in Great Britain by
Routledge
Taylor & Francis Group
2 Park Square
Milton Park, Abingdon
Oxon OX14 4RN

© 1997 by Taylor & Francis Group, LLC
Routledge is an imprint of Taylor & Francis Group

Printed in the United States of America on acid-free paper
10 9 8 7 6 5 4 3

International Standard Book Number-10: 90-5699-531-6 (Softcover)
International Standard Book Number-13: 978-90-5699-531-7 (Softcover)

Library of Congress Cataloging-in-Publication Data

Catalog record is available from the Library of Congress

Taylor & Francis Group
is the Academic Division of Informa plc.

Visit the Taylor & Francis Web site at
http://www.taylorandfrancis.com

and the Routledge Web site at
http://www.routledge-ny.com

To Michael, my family, and the women of Ndangane

Crossroads   a: A place where two or more roads meet   **b:** A place where different cultures meet **c:** A crucial point

Webster's II New Riverside Dictionary, 1984

CONTENTS

PREFACE

This book was written to paint a portrait of people who are infected with the human immunodeficiency virus (HIV) and people who have managed to avoid infection through sheer resourcefulness. Rather than report the findings of qualitative and quantitative research I conducted in Kaolack, Senegal, in 1991 and 1992, I have chosen to tell the story of the women *behind* the code names and statistics with the hope that students and other readers will gain a sense of the cultural context in which so many women struggle to make ends meet in the age of acquired immunodeficiency syndrome (AIDS). I also hope to give an identity and voice to my informants — people I interviewed and spent time with — who are women and mothers first, and prostitutes by necessity. The women portrayed here keep their profession a secret from their families and friends but abide by Senegalese law, which states that prostitution is legal for those who register with the police and undergo bimonthly health examinations. By registering, the women avoid arrest and take responsibility for their actions. Although they claim to be trapped by the social and political forces that have led them to enter prostitution, I argue here that they have taken control of their destinies in an inspiring fashion.

HIV has ravaged the African continent faster and earlier than any other in the world. For African countries, particularly in the east and central portions of the continent, HIV/AIDS has torn through villages and cities, disproportionately affecting men and women of working age, further harming an already suffering economy. In fact, the lack of sufficient resources for illness prevention and health care in general that preceded the epidemic clearly has hindered efforts to educate people about HIV and to care for those already infected.

In an attempt to demonstrate that serious efforts are being made to quell HIV transmission in the face of limited resources, this book provides insight into a predominantly Muslim and polygamous Subsaharan African country's response to the pandemic. More generally, its description of one sexually transmitted disease (STD) clinic's successful AIDS education campaign demonstrates that information presented in a culturally appropriate manner can indeed achieve the common goal of behavior change. My objective in minimizing the campaign itself while dedicating the majority of the book to women's lives is to reveal the complexity of bringing about such behavior and attitude change through relatively few informative presentations and words of safe-sex advice. I demonstrate that it is possible to identify and disseminate messages that will convince people to change their behaviors. But those messages must be carefully constructed and tested to ensure they give people sufficient reason for change that strikes a chord, reverberating throughout their daily decision-making processes.

Throughout this book I refer to my prostitute informants as women and as prostitutes, since that is the direct translation of the Wolof (Senegal's *lingua franca*) and French (Senegal's official language) words they use to describe themselves. I am aware that "commercial sex worker" is often favored as more politically correct but because this is the women's story, I use the women's words. The stories are typical of the women's situations but certainly not all-encompassing. Likewise, although the individual lives, circumstances, and issues discussed in this book resemble some of what has happened in other Senegalese cities, in other developing countries, and among disenfranchised women in developed countries, they should not be regarded as representative of the epidemic's toll on women everywhere. Instead, the lessons learned could be cautiously applied to other education efforts and analyses of the impact of AIDS on women in a variety of economic, social, and political contexts.

What is universal, however, is that AIDS affects every community to its core, while cultural factors influence the actual nature and even degree of its impact. For this reason, I believe this and countless other stories about the various faces of AIDS need to be told. Whereas many of the words and perceptions I include belong to the women, I wish to make it clear that my world view affected my reactions to what I witnessed and heard as I conducted research. To provide a more holistic view of the fieldwork process, I include descriptions of my attempts to make sense of my findings and observations.

It is for this and several other reasons that the image of *crossroads* is most appropriate. In the following pages I recount some of the situations that arose during my work with a group of women and clinic staff from cultures very different from my own. Coming from different directions, we met at a common point to share our concern about HIV prevention and the impact of HIV on women. The physical location of this meeting was Kaolack — Senegal's crossroads. It is a town where travelers and prostitutes converge and HIV transmission rates have soared among the prostitutes, primarily due to frequent travel by them and their partners. The time of the meeting was also a crossroads of sorts, a point at which the women were confronting the threat of AIDS head-on and making crucial decisions about the path they would follow. Aware that a wrong choice could result in infection and an early death, they were — and still are — weighing the costs and benefits of the sort of conscious and complex behavior change that deeply affects relationships and social roles.

To best illustrate the factors affecting the women throughout their lives and during AIDS-related decision-making processes, I have divided the book into seven chapters. The introduction sets the scene for the study, providing background information on the process that led me to focus on this group of women and the theoretical and methodological approaches that guided my

research. Chapter one describes the context of the study, high-
lighting the historic and cultural factors, including the nature of
the AIDS epidemic in Senegal, that shape the lives of women.
Chapter two focuses more closely on life for prostitutes in
Kaolack through a close look at their literal and figurative place
in their community.

The subsequent four chapters are arranged around themes
that emerged as I analyzed the prostitutes' statements, life histories, and relationships. Chapter three focuses on one STD
clinic's AIDS education campaign and the women who responded most enthusiastically and visibly to the call for a
community-wide effort to curb HIV transmission. Chapter
four examines the influence of religion on the prostitutes and
their attempts to balance their devotion to Islam with their
economic need to practice prostitution — regarded as a sin
commensurate with adultery even if the prostitute is not married. Chapter five explores prevailing Senegalese health
behaviors and perceptions about the categorization of AIDS
within the traditional health belief system. Chapter six re-
counts the stories of women who have had difficulty coping
with the blows life has dealt them, and marvels at their resil-
ience in the battle against AIDS.

The final chapter puts the issues raised throughout this
book into perspective. One predominant issue is the recognition that there is heterogeneity within groups commonly held
to be homogeneous and that the characteristics that separate
group members are as relevant to HIV prevention as those
that unite them. Similar is the need to acknowledge the multiple factors affecting individuals and groups of individuals. In
this light, understanding the context of prostitution requires
attention to economic, political, and social factors. Finally, despite the grand scale on which AIDS is changing lives world-
wide, it remains essential to document individual efforts
toward the goal of behavior change, which in the era of AIDS
often requires and perpetuates increased control over one's
health and future.

ACKNOWLEDGMENTS

The research for this study was supported by Family Health International (FHI) with funds from the United States Agency for International Development (USAID). Partial support was provided by the United States Information Agency (USIA) through the Fulbright United States Graduate Fellowship Program. The views expressed in this book do not necessarily reflect those of FHI, USAID, or USIA.

Special thanks go to my husband Michael Renaud for his invaluable support, patience, and editing skills; and to my mother Maxine Stanoff Lewis for her encouragement and visualization of the best way to tell the women's stories. I also wish to thank my father Byron Lewis; my grandparents Evelyn Stanoff, Harry Stanoff, and Brooks Lewis; and my brother Barry Lewis for always being there for me. Thanks also to Liz Kresse for literature search assistance; Carol Maus for her much-needed editing assistance; and my inspirational dissertation committee: Margaret Boone, PhD, William Leap, PhD, and Dolores Koenig, PhD.

Grateful acknowledgment goes to Dr. Souleymane Mboup and the staff and prostitutes at the Centre MST in Kaolack, without whose acceptance and assistance this book would not have been possible. Finally, I wish to express my gratitude to Ibrahima Sow of Kaolack, who provided me with a family and friendship I will not forget.

Introduction

Fatou leaned against the wall of her hut, her legs outstretched on her bed—a foam mattress propped on two truck tires. The walls were cardboard, hung on the thatch structure for a smooth interior. Over the cardboard were pieces of cloth hung like so many patches of a quilt. She pulled her bright yellow and red *pagne*—a long, rectangular cloth wrapped around her—down from under her arms to her hips and cooled her dark neck and chest with a plastic fan while chewing on a *cure dent*, a small stick used for cleaning teeth.

Outside, men selling perfume and clothes shuffled in blue and green rubber thongs through the dirt, silently advertising their wares. Because of the heat, few women were outside their huts, and the men passed through Ndangane without taking the energy to yell out for customers, knowing it would be a slow day. Even the goats and cats, usually wandering around in search of food, had taken quiet shelter in the shade of the women's huts.

Fatou and I relaxed as she answered my questions about her life and how she had entered prostitution. Men and money.

1

Men in her life had failed to support her and, needing money to
clothe and feed her aging mother and young children, she drew
on the only resource she possessed: her body. "Being a prostitute is like being a leaf that is blown by the wind into a hole,"
she said, glancing at me with her right eye. Her left eye remained lodged in the corner closest to her nose. When she saw
I did not understand, she took her *cure dent* out of her mouth,
leaned over the side of her bed and dug a hole in her dirt floor.
She tossed the stick into the hole, sat up, and crossed her arms.
"See," she tilted her head toward the stick. "A leaf in a hole
can't get out by itself."

Out of the background noise of muffled conversations and
footsteps, we heard a loud voice summoning assistance.
Rhama, one of Fatou's best friends, was announcing that her
client refused to wear a condom. Fatou quickly stood up and
pulled her *pagne* over her chest, tying it tightly above her right
breast. She slipped on her blue thongs and grabbed a wooden
club propped in the corner of the hut. As she stepped outside
she joined several other women approaching Rhama's hut,
yelling at the hidden man. He peeked out at the crowd from
behind a dark blue and green cloth hanging in the doorway.
Instantly, he let the cloth drop. Rhama stepped out from behind the cloth, holding her untied *pagne* over her breasts and
smiled thankfully at her colleagues. She stepped back in,
pulled the cloth inside the hut and closed the metal door behind her. The other women returned to their huts and Fatou to
hers, where she put her club in its corner, kicked off her
thongs, lay down on her bed, and fanned herself again.

****

This book is a story of solidarity and of independence. It is a
story of life and of death and of that state in-between. It is a
story of women's dependency on men and of their ability to
gain power and control in spite of men. Most importantly, it is
a story of the women of Ndangane, who have become prosti-

tutes for economic survival, only to discover that they have much more at stake than their families' support, their next meal, and their ability to buy beautiful *pagnes* and a steady supply of *cure dents*.

In their effort to survive in a world dominated by men they have found that, while prostitution brings them autonomy, it is almost impossible to leave the profession on their own. They have also found that selling sex as a survival strategy can become a "death strategy" in the age of acquired immunodeficiency syndrome (AIDS) (Schoepf 1988:217). That is why Fatou keeps her club nearby, and why she is willing to use it to enforce condom use. If she does not help Rhama convince her client to wear a condom, Rhama may accept unsafe sex in exchange for money she desperately needs. If Rhama accepts, the man has won, and the group of women who share huts in Ndangane have lost a battle in their fight against human immunodeficiency virus (HIV) transmission. They have also lost in their battle to gain some sort of control in a world where they see themselves as having very few options. They do not think they can leave prostitution on their own, but within their small community, those who desire have achieved a degree of control over their professional sexual relations, their finances, and their health.

Fatou, Rhama, and the other prostitutes in this dirty neighborhood on the outskirts of Kaolack, Senegal's third largest town, point to men when asked how and why they entered the profession. Fathers did not allow them to go to school. Fathers forced them to marry against their wishes. Husbands beat them. Husbands took other wives with whom they did not get along. Husbands died. Ex-husbands did not pay mandatory child support. Grown sons did not assume financial support of their widowed or divorced mothers, as tradition dictates.

Talk to other Senegalese about prostitutes and they tell a different story. They say women choose prostitution out of "vice," they are corrupt and sinful and can never be "converted." They

insist that the women could find another source of income—
other women in the same situation have—while the reality is
that these women tried and could not.

When I first moved to Kaolack and began talking with people about prostitution in the age of AIDS, I was determined to
uncover the "truth," to somehow scientifically prove whether
the women did have other economic options. After much effort and attempted analysis I decided there were more important questions to answer. I needed to examine why different
factions saw the situation as they did and believed what they
believed, rather than search for an empirical truth.

Coming from a middle class American family, never deprived of food or clothes, I could relate to the people ready to
dismiss the prostitutes with the judgmental brush of a hand.
Knowing this, I tried to relate to the prostitutes. The stories
they told shed light on the complexity of economic and social
dependence, and on the even more complicated relations between men and women in a "modern" Islamic society. That
they believed they had no other economic options was the pivotal issue. That they have responded so quickly and forcefully
to the threat of AIDS to their economic and physical well-
being was the fact I felt compelled to document. That they are
so similar to me and women throughout the world is the issue
that renders their story so remarkable.

CONFRONTING BIASES

Before I met Fatou, Rhama, and the prostitutes in Ndangane,
and before I received funding to conduct my dissertation research on AIDS and Senegalese women, I was certain that I
would not focus on prostitutes. Because of my biases and
because most AIDS research—if on women at all—excluded
non-prostitute women, I drafted a proposal to explore the
knowledge and practices of women not involved in prostitution. I traveled from the U.S. to Dakar in June 1990 to further

define my plan by interviewing several health care professionals, including Dr. Souleymane Mboup, a professor of bacteri-
ology and virology at the University of Dakar and head of the
AIDS research program at Hôpital Dantec.

Upon reviewing my proposal, Dr. Mboup immediately and
strongly suggested that I change my strategy. There was a
need to interview women, he acknowledged, but the most dire
need was to uncover the dynamics of HIV transmission
among the people most at risk: prostitutes. Nothing had been
written about them in Senegal, save clinical reports about their
extremely high rate of infection. The HIV infection rate of
prostitutes in Kaolack was and remains the highest in the
country, leading to his interest in discerning the "culture of
prostitution" in Kaolack.

Acknowledging that qualitative data can contribute significantly in the design of effective education campaigns, he and
other AIDS researchers told me they were interested in an ethnographic study that would explain the dynamics of HIV
transmission and prevention among Kaolack prostitutes. He
explained I could join his team of AIDS researchers by working with the staff at the STD clinic in Kaolack, who had the
most contact with prostitutes seeking medical treatment and
AIDS information.

I agreed to consider his offer because I wanted my study to
respond directly to the needs of local researchers, policy makers, and women facing the threat of HIV infection. A few days
later I drove with a missionary friend, Miriam, to Kaolack to
visit the Centre des Maladies Sexuelles Transmissibles (Center
for Sexually Transmitted Diseases, referred to as "the clinic").
We introduced ourselves to the staff, then the head nurse and
laboratory technician took us on a tour of the town. The tour
included a visit to Ndangane, a neighborhood where many of
the prostitutes work and live.

When we walked into the work place of the prostitutes, a few
women who saw us approach talked briefly to the technician
and head nurse, pulled their two best chairs into the middle of a

dusty, shadeless courtyard and said that Miriam and I should sit down. Bordering the courtyard were rows of thatch huts, probably sixty of them in an area the size of a square block. At the end of one row of huts was the latrine, a hole in the ground bordered by an eye-level, thatch fence. As we sat down, a crowd gathered to observe us. It was comprised predominantly of women, although some children ducked between their legs to get a glimpse of us, and some men milled around on the fringes waiting for the women to leave us and attend to them. I did not know if we were supposed to say something or not, so I looked at Miriam, who smiled in silence, expecting something to happen. I did the same, though I found it hard to smile surrounded by strangers saying things I did not understand.

As I waited and took it all in, I could smell alcohol, incense, and perfume, intermingled and intensified by the heat. I was thankful to be sitting down, as I could not focus on anything for the rainbow of colors whirling around me. I became dizzier when some of the women began to dance and sing, but kept smiling to show my appreciation for the entertainment. The women chided each other, shaking their rear-ends and pulling their long robes up to their knees so they could move more easily. One woman danced over to me, turned her back to me and shook herself a foot from my face, to the cheers of the audience. It was all I could do to keep smiling.

Suddenly, a hand holding two cold Cokes came out of the crowd. I felt relieved beyond words, but thought it would have made a great commercial. Miriam offered money to the woman who brought them, but the woman graciously declined. Miriam leaned over and told me that this was a true sign of hospitality, especially given the high cost of refrigeration and soft drinks relative to people's income.

Although Miriam kept smiling, I could tell she was as overwhelmed as I was—me by the actions and words I did not understand, and she by the actions and words she understood but had not seen before despite her ten years of teaching religion and heading development projects in Senegal. Later she would tell me she was glad to have the experience once to get a glimpse of life for the prostitutes, but only once.

When the women quieted down, the doctor and head nurse explained that I was visiting Kaolack and planned to return to conduct research on health issues. Because there had been another white female researcher in their midst in 1989, the prostitutes were used to being interviewed and said they would be cooperative. We said goodbye and drove back to the clinic. When I told the staff more about my proposed study, they said they were interested and would assist however they could. When I asked them to think about the issues they wanted to explore and specific questions they would want asked through interviews, they eagerly started writing. Before I left the clinic, they handed me their ideas. Looking at the page, I was surprised to find a long list of equipment and supplies they needed. Miriam was not.

When I returned to the United States I revised my proposal and submitted it to several funding sources. My new focus was to assess the extent to which the clinic's AIDS education campaign was reaching prostitute women in Kaolack and how various cultural factors were impeding or facilitating the transmission of HIV. With letters from Dr. Mboup and other prominent researchers testifying to their interest in this topic and support of my proposal, I was able to get funding.

COLLECTING AND ANALYZING DATA

In June 1991, a year after my first visit, I returned to Senegal with funding as a Fulbright Fellow and as an AIDSTECH (AIDS Technology) Fellow with Family Health International. I lived in Dakar for two months while I studied Wolof, spoken by the majority of Senegalese, and interviewed American, French, and Senegalese AIDS researchers about AIDS education campaigns

and the country's medical system. I visited Kaolack several
times before moving there in August.

From August 1991 through May 1992, I lived in Kaolack.
During that time, I conducted research through participant
observation; numerous informal interviews with clinic staff,
health care practitioners, friends and neighbors; focus group
discussions with prostitutes; and two phases of interviews
with Senegalese women. For the first phase, I held semi-
structured interviews with every consenting prostitute and
non-prostitute who attended the STD clinic for examinations
and STD treatment during a one-month period. I also interviewed non-prostitutes, who comprised one-third of the total
sample. In all, I interviewed one hundred women: sixty-eight
were prostitutes and thirty-two were non-prostitutes.

The second phase of interviews included informal life history interviews with twenty prostitutes interviewed during
the first phase: ten of these women were prostitutes who
worked in Ndangane and ten were prostitutes who worked in
bars and hotels in town. Many of these women and other people with whom I spent a great deal of time became key informants, individuals whom I interviewed formally and
informally on several occasions over time to gain a better understanding of their perspectives, knowledge, and daily lives.

The questionnaire used during the first phase of interviews
was divided into two main sections. The first focused on demographic factors and sought information about each woman's age, marital status, ethnicity, religion, education, living
situation, number of children, and use of birth control. The second section focused on the woman's knowledge, attitudes,
and practices regarding AIDS. First, however, I asked each
woman general questions about social and health problems
affecting her, her family, and her country to assess the issues
most prevalent in her thoughts and to see if she would mention AIDS on her own. Responses indicated the prevalence of
concerns about AIDS and, simultaneously, helped me assess

other areas of interviewee concern. This approach, modeled after Forster and Furley's (1988) survey on attitudes and knowledge about AIDS in Uganda, revealed interviewees' perceptions of AIDS-related risk and the degree to which concern has affected their likelihood to seek more knowledge about AIDS and to take measures to protect themselves from HIV infection.

Once AIDS became a topic in the interview (either through the woman's initiative or mine), I asked questions to assess the informant's knowledge of AIDS transmission, prevention, symptoms, and services offered through traditional and modern health care practitioners. I also posed questions such as: "What kinds of people get AIDS?" to determine who is stigmatized and why; "How is it similar to/different from other diseases?"; and "What kinds of treatment are there for it?". These data were used to place issues into domains as the women presented them (Bernard 1988:229; Spradley 1972). For other questions, I read lists of possible answers to the women after they gave an initial response to the question. This technique enabled me to determine if my perceptions were correct, to add to the list of domains, and to identify the various facets of each category.

To determine whether formal and informal channels of health care education had an impact on promoting AIDS awareness and "safe sex" activity (Wilson et al. 1988), I elicited information such as the type of AIDS, sex, and health education informants received at school and through organizations such as family planning clinics and community groups. I also asked whether they have changed their behavior as a result of their exposure to the media, traditional health care providers, and people living with AIDS.

The two goals of the second phase of interviews were to learn more about the women's lifestyles, life decisions, and world views and to elaborate on and identify additional domains. To this end, I asked the women to tell me their life histories; to describe the most important thing that ever happened to them; to list types of things belonging to domains (such as types of clients, types of prostitutes, ways to convince clients to engage in safe sex, ways to make money, and ways to hide their work from relatives); and to discuss their roles as prostitutes, mothers, daughters, sisters, and wives.

I elicited informants' economic histories to gain more insight about circumstances leading women to engage in prostitution and other income-earning activities and to assess how they view their work and their position in society. I also requested reproductive histories to document similarities in their reproductive choices, marital patterns, living situations, and social roles.

To arrive at an understanding of issues important to my informants, I followed Spradley's (1972) model of ethnoscientific inquiry in urban settings, which is divided into five stages: hypothesizing that certain areas are culturally significant; recording a corpus of relevant statements in the language of informants; examining the corpus of statements for possible domains, question frames and substitution frames; eliciting the categories of culturally-relevant domains, which results in a folk taxonomy or native-category system for identifying significant objects in the subculture; and discovering the semantic principles of a number of domains. I incorporated these steps into data collection and analysis in order to interpret data on AIDS-related beliefs and behaviors in an appropriate cultural context.

Gladwin's (1989) method of decision-tree modeling guided my choice of questions to determine the circumstances surrounding the women's decisions on two major issues: whether to enforce condom use in various situations and how to earn sufficient income. The answers revealed the women's reasons for behaving in certain ways and, by extension, helped predict how they might act in the future. The model allows for the testing of initial hypotheses and could be employed in the designing of HIV education programs that are sensitive to factors affecting decisions about sexual behavior.

I incorporated a medical anthropological approach to the study of the Senegalese medical system, viewing it as a cultural system (Yoder 1980). As Kleinman (1978) suggests, obtaining information about the beliefs and healing activities that take place in popular, folk, and professional arenas sheds light on health perceptions and communal relations. In conducted interviews with clinic staff, prostitutes, and male and female informants in my neighborhood. The results led me to an understanding of the interactions between health concepts and healing activities at home, in the huts of *marabouts*, and in dorctors' offices. From this understanding, I was able to analyzer the place of AIDS in Senegalese belief and behavioural systems. People's ways of dealing with illness, including AIDS, are directly linked to their beliefs about illness causality, diagnosis, and treatment (Frake 1961; Ingstad 1990; Yoder 1980).

To analyze data accumulated during the first phase of interviews, I coded the women's responses to create a database of demographic characteristics and ran additional cross tabulations to determine whether personal characteristic variables explored in the first part of the questionnaire correlated with answers to specific AIDS questions comprising the second part of the questionnaire. I assessed patterns and consensus, or lack thereof, within and between the two groups.

I used these data as a frame of reference for interpreting responses to the in-depth interviews to determine the extent to which responses in the second phase elaborated on themes raised in the first. This involved identifying examples from the second phase of interviews that illustrate and explain these themes and, in some cases, shed a different light on preliminary impressions. Through content analysis of informants' responses as text, I obtained a sense of the meaning underlying the language they chose when they responded to questions, expanded on issues, recounted life histories (Agar 1980; Leap

1991) and categorized types of diseases, people, and occupations (Frake 1961; Spradley 1972).

In addition, I evaluated life histories to discern where individual circumstances and perceptions interfaced with the more general characteristics of the larger sample. I also identified specific factors that were consistent within this smaller sample. More specifically, the information from in-depth interviews with prostitutes enabled me to understand life in Kaolack from the point of view of female prostitutes in their roles as women, mothers, daughters, sisters, and prostitutes. I examined differences between and similarities among prostitutes' perspectives and those of their non-prostitute counterparts, who shared characteristics, such as age, ethnicity, religion, education, and motherhood.

To analyze the data obtained through observations, I studied the notes I took while at the clinic, conducting formal and informal interviews, facilitating focus group discussions, listening to health care lectures, attending medical researchers' meetings, and observing day-to-day events. Informal interviews with health care professionals aided me in monitoring the issues they deal with on a daily basis and the ways they attempt to effectively educate clinic clients. Material from focus group discussions with prostitutes helped me uncover areas of agreement and dissent about general health issues, preventative behavior, and perceptions of AIDS risk among prostitutes. Meetings with health care professionals in Kaolack and Dakar helped me assess how cultural factors come into play in the creation of education strategies, how health care professionals talk about the issues confronting them, and how discoveries in the clinic and laboratory translate into active strategies in the public education realm (Airhihenbuwa 1989). AIDS researchers' accounts about the changes that have taken place since the advent of AIDS helped me understand the types of societal and structural responses that have occurred during the last decade.

A PROFILE OF THE STUDY SAMPLE

To obtain a profile of women in the study sample, I accumulated demographic data to gain a sense of the diversity within the study sample, to assess differences and similarities among prostitutes and non-prostitutes, and to compare findings about women in the study sample to information about Senegalese women in general.

In terms of educational level, the number of years women in the study spent in school ranges from zero to twelve and the average among all the women is 2.3 years. Fifty-eight percent of the women had no education at all and three women had the maximum of twelve years. The majority of the women (sixty-two percent) did not speak French, the country's national language. However, one third of the women knew how to read and write; half of these women were prostitutes. This is higher than in the general population in Senegal, where eighteen percent of the women can read and write.

Economic activities were especially important in revealing the women's sources of income and their economic decisions. Within this study, all but one of the women lived in an urban setting and the majority of non-prostitutes considered themselves housewives. Of thirty-two non-prostitutes, twenty-seven did not work outside their homes and all but one who worked outside of the home were married. Approximately thirty percent of the prostitutes earned money through a second source, usually the commerce of goods such as food, clothes, perfume, and jewelry. Other work included doing laundry, hairstyling, and working in restaurants and bars. Analysis of the women's ethnicity revealed that thirty percent were Serer and thirty-eight percent were Wolof, resembling the ethnic make-up of Kaolack (Nelson 1974). These groups were followed by Fulbe, Toucouleur, Mandinka, Diola, Laobe, Soninke, and Maure. Laobe is the name of the Fulbe's wood-working class, but

members of the caste and others often referred to Laobe as
Laobe rather than as Fulbe.

These demographic data indicate that the study sample represented the variety of characteristics among Senegalese
women in Kaolack and reveals a general lack of AIDS knowledge among women not specifically targeted with AIDS prevention information. The sample of prostitutes is especially
varied and demonstrative of the range within the group insofar as age, economic activities, ethnic background and religion
is concerned. Most significant is that, despite these differences, knowledge about AIDS and reported enforcement of
condom use is extremely high throughout the group of prostitutes registered at the clinic in Kaolack.

THE MAIN PLAYERS IN THIS BOOK

When analyzing the life histories I accumulated and the observations I made, I grouped the women according to the characteristics that seemed most significant in their lives and
relations with their families, clinic staff, and each other. I drew
on these characteristics to form the chapters of this book,
which explore the ways in which the women cope with their
lives as prostitutes and their fear of HIV infection. Although
oversimplifying aspects of individuals' personalities and activities could diminish their individuality, many of the groupings mirror their own groupings of themselves and each other,
as will become evident in the following chapters. The wom-
en's names have been changed to common Senegalese names.
While specific statistics and findings of my research are published elsewhere (Lewis 1993; Renaud 1993), the stories recounted are drawn from my personal experiences while
conducting quantitative and qualitative research. They have
but one purpose: to give voices to the women and faces to the
statistics.

The names and brief descriptions of the main players follow. I do not list all of the prostitutes, because they are introduced as the stories unfold. I also do not list the names of most clinic staff to avoid confusion and because some members are presented in a negative light; in all cases, I portray them from the perspective of the prostitutes who attended the clinic.

Michael—It was during the two months I spent in Dakar prior to moving to Kaolack that I met and began seeing Michael, the Army Attaché at the American Embassy. As my boyfriend, my anchor, and my sounding board, he became a pivotal part of my life during and following my fieldwork. When we returned to the United States we were married.

Youma—Youma, a young woman still in high school, lived around the corner from me in Kaolack. She became my friend, confidant, Wolof tutor, and a key informant on issues affecting non-prostitute women.

Ibrahima—Introduced to me by his niece, who was introduced to me by a mutual American friend who had lived in Senegal, Ibrahima was my adopted uncle and a key informant about life for married men in Senegal. A devout Muslim with several children and a working wife, he offered the perspective of someone critical of prostitutes and the men who frequent them.

Mbodj—Ibrahima told Mbodj to leave his two wives and four children in his village forty miles away in order to guard my house. Eager to please Ibrahima, who had done him many favors, and knowing the pay would be good, Mbodj agreed to help out. We became close during our many conversations in the shade of my cashew tree. He shared with me information about rural life and male/female relations from the point of view of an uneducated Muslim man and played host to Michael and me during our many trips to visit him and his family in their village.

Maria—As the better French speaker of the two nurses at the clinic (she is a nurse and the other is an assistant nurse),

Maria became my translator during the first phase of interviews. Following that she remained a close friend and informant about life as the second wife in a polygamous household.

Ibra—A former social worker at the STD clinic, Ibra offered
insight about the nature of prostitution in Senegal and the
stigma associated with its practice. His dedication to the prostitutes in Ndangane provided me with a glimpse of what educated Senegalese could contribute to the women's cause and
the fight against AIDS.

The STD Clinic Doctor—Trained in Dakar and supported in
part by Harvard University's AIDS research program, the
clinic doctor was an invaluable authority on health care in
Senegal and the dynamics of STD and AIDS prevalence rates.
As an educated single male in his mid-thirties, he spoke to me
of the advantages and disadvantages of marriage and the nature of male/female relations in Senegal.

The STD Clinic Head Nurse—An educated woman with the
second-most powerful position at the clinic (the doctor was in
charge of the clinic, while she was in charge of the other two
nurses and made many decisions affecting the prostitutes fre-
quenting the clinic), the head nurse informed me about the difficulty of balancing a successful career with a monogamous
marriage. She also patiently explained the structure and function of the clinic and the difficulties of working with prostitutes.

The STD Laboratory Technician—The technician was corrup-
tion personified (by all accounts). He contributed the perspective of someone who benefitted from the prostitutes' situation
by selling them donated condoms and arguing against attempts to train them for other professions.

The STD Social Worker—Although sensitive to the prostitutes' troubled lives and extremely knowledgeable about the
dynamics of prostitution in Senegal, the social worker was reluctant to extend support to the prostitutes beyond the con-
fines of his office. The prostitutes compared him disfavorably
to Ibra, who was always eager to help them.

Fatou—Fatou was very active in promoting condom use among the women in Ndangane and was a proponent of the single lifestyle for independent women.

Khady—Of all the prostitutes, I spent the most amount of time with Khady, who volunteered her time as translator, story-teller, and close friend. Like Fatou, she was one of the leading players in the network of women in Ndangane who took charge of their lives in the age of AIDS by requiring that their clients wear condoms, providing condoms to their colleagues, and advocating on the prostitutes' behalf at the clinic and police station.

Rhama—Like Khady, Rhama was a key informant who explained the intricacies of life as a prostitute and of condom negotiation with clients.

1

The Context of Women's Lives

*Addressing prostitution as "behavior" and ignoring its psychosocial causes
and context ... provides no guidance or insight into the long-term ramifica-
tions of the AIDS pandemic for the spectrum of personal relationships between and among men and women.*

(DeZalduondo 1991)

A BRIEF HISTORY OF SENEGAL

Senegal, Wolof for "our boat" (*sunu gaal*), is located on the
west coast of the African continent, and extends three hundred miles inland from the Atlantic. About half way down the
coast is the Cap Vert peninsula, the westernmost point in
Africa. Senegal shares borders with Mauritania, Mali, Guinea,
Guinea Bissau, and the Gambia. Senegal covers almost 76,000
square miles, most of which are flat plains of savanna, stretch-
ing across the continent just south of the Sahara desert.

Senegal's primary ethnic groups are the Wolof, Serer, Lebou, Toucouleur, Fulbe (which the Senegalese refer to as Peulh), Sarakolle, Mandinka, Bambara, and Diola. Members of these ethnic groups, particularly the Fulbe, Mandinka and Bambara, also live in neighboring countries due to the arbitrary colonial boundaries cutting across ancient empires (Nelson 1974). Wolof (42%), Fulbe and Toucouleur (23%), Serer (14%), Diola (6%), and Mandinka (5%) are the five largest ethnic groups in Senegal (Nelson 1974).

As indicated above, the Fulbe and Toucouleur are often grouped together because they share a common language, Pulaar. Still, they retain cultural differences, most notably in their religious affiliation and means of supporting themselves; the Toucouleur are often sedentary farmers, whereas the Fulbe are more likely to lead a nomadic lifestyle as cattle herders. The Wolof have played a dominant role in the country's political system and their language is the *lingua franca*, spoken by eighty percent of the Senegalese (Nelson 1974). However, the Wolof have assimilated many of the characteristics of their neighboring ethnic groups, as is evidenced in their language and culture. (For additional history, see Nelson 1974 and Gellar 1982.)

Islam has played a large role in the lives of people from the majority of the country's ethnic groups and has often presented those from the lower classes with opportunities not previously available. In the eleventh century, Muslims reached Senegal and the leader of the Toucouleur converted to the Islamic faith. Most of his followers did likewise. Not until the fifteenth century, however, did Islam begin to penetrate the entire area and take on characteristics of Senegalese culture during a period of increasing colonial dominance (Creevey 1991).

The first Portuguese traders arrived in Senegal in the fifteenth century in search of slaves. Originally a local operation, the slave trade was quickly transformed into an international one. In addition to the Portuguese, the Dutch, British, and French became active participants in the export of Senegalese men, women, and children. Until the end of the sixteenth century, the Senegambia region was the largest supplier of slaves to Europe. Still, traders continued to export slaves from Senegal and neighboring countries until the end of the eighteenth century (Gellar 1982).

The domination of the Senegalese by the French throughout the nineteenth century destroyed the existing Senegalese social, political, and economic structures. Although the slave trade ended in the early 1800's, other forms of trade took its place (Carr 1985). The most popular commodity was gum Arabic, extracted from trees and used to set the color of textile dyes in the booming European textile industry. Peanuts eventually became Senegal's primary crop, with much demand in Europe, where they were used as an oil base for soaps and cooking (Carr 1985).

In 1959, Senegal began negotiating with France for independence as a constitutional unit of the Mali Federation, comprised of Senegal and former French Soudan. The Mali Federation became independent on April 4, 1960. Soon thereafter, Senegal seceded and declared itself a republic, rendering it separate and autonomous. The Federation broke up in August of the same year. By the end of September 1960, Senegal had its own constitution and a seat in the United Nations. Led from 1960 to 1980 by Leopold Senghor, the poet-president from the Parti Socialiste, the country gained recognition as one of the most stable and least repressive in Africa. After a long period of single-party rule, a movement for a multiparty system in the 1970's produced eleven opposition parties by 1982 (Gellar 1982).

Senegal's post-independence administrations took control of the administrative structures, legal system, and police powers of the French colonial state. Instead of destroying these institutions, however, Senegalese leaders Africanized them (Gellar 1982). They divided the country, comprised of 13,000 villages, into new administrative districts, creating seven regions, twenty-eight departments, and eighty-five *arrondissements* (wards) (Gellar 1982). This restructuring included the allocation of more power to local governments and the creation of councils that govern activities in rural areas (Gellar 1982).

Despite these advances and the maintenance of political stability, the Senegalese economy never took off after independence as predicted (Creevey 1991). The market for peanuts fell significantly and the export of agricultural products decreased. Overall industrial production was less in 1988 than in 1982. Phosphate exports, however, increased substantially, and the service sector (particularly activities related to tourism) also grew. Although tourism is now the largest source of national income, it has recently declined due to political conflicts in the Casamance. An area in the southern part of the country where beautiful beaches and national parks are located, Casamance has been a popular tourist destination (Creevey 1991).

Importantly, poverty remains a major problem in Senegal. A United Nations report ranked Senegal 112 out of 130 countries in an index of human development based on literacy, per capita income, and life expectancy. The average annual per capita income is around 150,000 francs (referred to as Communauté Français Africain, or CFA), which is approximately six hundred U.S. dollars (Pillsbury 1990:27). In 1965, life expectancy was forty years. Today, the average life span is forty-nine years for women and forty-six for men (Pillsbury 1990).

A BRIEF HISTORY OF WOMEN IN SENEGAL

With the arrival of French traders in the fifteenth and sixteenth centuries, many Senegalese women, particularly among the Wolof and Lebou people, became involved with European men who traveled for trade. The male traders lived most often on the islands of Saint Louis and Gorée. Attracted by the striking and ambitious Senegalese women known for their acuity as traders, many of the men took them as wives, adopting local marriage customs. Men who married slaves purchased their freedom as a wedding present (Brooks 1976:33). Wives of these traders were referred to as *signares*, the French version of the Portuguese *senhora*. They were respected and provided their husbands as many social and economic benefits as they received. They were regarded as excellent hostesses, and often earned income through trade of their own. Brooks reports that women who unsuccessfully tried to become *signares* may have "lapsed into casual prostitution" and contributed to the spread of STDs (Brooks 1976:34).

This is not to say that women did not already obtain positions of prestige in traditional society. They definitely did, although women's status was not homogeneous across ethnic boundaries (Gellar 1982:4). Despite scant information, Mandinka oral traditions refer to "queens" in the land that was to become Senegal. Other evidence indicates that some women, especially among the Wolof and Lebou, ruled west African villages. In addition to their leadership skills they, like the women of Saint Louis and Gorée, were known for their wealth acquired through trade (Brooks 1976). According to Gellar, women living in the Casamance enjoyed a higher status than did their counterparts up north, due to the equal participation of men and women in agricultural production (Gellar 1982).

As early as the seventeenth century, several prominent women traders reportedly resided in Rufisque, the first port and trading center established in Senegal located about fifteen miles from present-day Dakar. Later, in the eighteenth and nineteenth centuries, many female traders lived in the Senegambia region and the Upper Guinea Coast. The largest group was in Senegal to accommodate European traders in Saint Louis and Gorée, who outnumbered their counterparts elsewhere in west Africa (Brooks 1976).

Despite the success achieved by some Senegalese women, they have always been second to men as dictated by traditional, colonial, and Muslim ideologies (Creevey 1991). Some traditional groups may have been matrilineal, but, as among the Serer, inheritance went to a woman's brother, not to her directly. Today, most ethnic groups in Senegal operate under a patrilineal system (Carr 1985).

Under European control, Senegalese political, social, and economic structures were made to resemble those in France, where women did not have a say in political issues or have the right to vote until the twentieth century. Consequently, early assimilation attempts completely ignored the traditional roles of Senegalese women as agriculturalists, traders, and, in some cases, household heads. Development projects also tailored training programs and equipment donations to the needs and work of men, who were seen as the country's sole breadwinners and decision-makers (Creevey 1991).

When Islam began to spread throughout Senegal, it sanctioned women's inferior status, but also granted them some new privileges. Changes in Wolof women's roles over the years is especially evident in written documentation and oral history (Creevey 1991). Islam granted women the right to the money their husbands gave to them at marriage (their bride price), which they could spend as they chose. They gained complete control over their own earnings. For the first time, they inherited land and property from their fathers, although they received half of that allocated their brothers (Koran 4:12). When a husband died, one tenth of the inheritance was divided among the wives and the rest was given to the children, who were expected to help support their mothers.

Under traditional Islamic law, men may marry up to four women if they can treat them fairly and equitably (Koran 4:4). A man can divorce a wife at will but should have serious cause. A woman can only be granted divorce by a court if she proves her husband irresponsible. Testimony of one man, however, is equal to that of two women (Creevey 1991).

Islam was "Senegalized" when it penetrated the country in that women were not forced to wear veils or put into seclusion. They still moved about freely, traveling alone, and dressing in bright, attractive *boubous* (loose-fitting, floor-length robes). Insofar as political and religious involvement was concerned, Muslim Senegalese women had fewer rights than their counterparts in other countries. Still, according to Creevey, Senegalese animist and Christian women were no better off socially than Muslim women (1991).

During the twentieth century, as women in France were gaining status, the French granted women in Senegal increased involvement in politics. After Senegal's independence, the 1960's and 1970's saw the creation of additional civil rights protecting women. Women were granted the right to vote, hold public office, earn equal pay for equal work, and receive any social benefits the state provided, including membership in state cooperatives.

One of the most significant reforms was the 1972 *Code de la Famille* (Family Code), which put in place protective laws for women not advocated by Muslim law. These laws allowed women to have a say in whether their marriages would be polygamous or monogamous, required men to provide a reason for divorce before obtaining a court agreement, and obligated men to provide financial support to divorced wives. However, the continuing problem is that men have not consistently complied with their legal responsibilities (Creevey 1991).

During the last decade, a number of women's rights groups have emerged in Senegal. Many prominent women have written about and fought for equality at home and in the workplace (Creevey 1991). Despite their right to hold public office at the national, regional, and local level, few women have been elected or appointed. Although women are politically active, it is usually within their own associations. Consequently, they continue to lack access to the government institutions and organizations that control the economic resources of the society (Creevey 1991).

Inequality persists at the household level. If a married woman commits adultery, both she and her partner are punished. If a married man commits adultery, he is punished only if the act took place in his home. His partner is not punished. Men also retain the right to legally forbid wives to work outside the home (Pillsbury 1990).

THE NATURE OF ISLAM IN SENEGAL: WOMEN ARE A STEP BELOW

Roughly ninety percent of Senegalese identify themselves as Muslim (Morgan 1984). Although there are vast differences between countries where Islam is observed, its fundamental tenets transcend cultural and geographic variation, and are expressed through the five pillars of Islam: declaring that there is but one God and Mohammed is his prophet; making a pilgrimage to Mecca (if financially possible); giving alms; fasting during the month of Ramadan; and praying five times a day (Nelson 1974). Muslim men are accorded many more rights than are women, whose observance is more restricted. This is evidenced by the fact that only post-menopausal women are permitted in mosques during prayer time and no women are allowed to enter the mosque while they are menstruating. Women may pray, but usually do so at home. These and other traditions are spelled out in Islam's indispensable documents: the Koran, which contains the words that God spoke through his prophet, Mohammed, and the *hadith*, which is an account of the prophet's teachings and deeds. Together, these two documents comprise the Sunna tradition of Islam, which is the only form found in Senegal (Nelson 1974).

Islam has no clergy or ordained priests. It has teachers and leaders, referred to as *marabouts* by the French and as *serigne* by the Wolof. Each mosque has an appointed chief *marabout* (*imam*), who is chosen by the community and serves for life.

Marabouts are said to be saintly men with charismatic qualities that help them acquire many followers. *Marabouts* also preside over religious functions and feasts, lead prayers, and teach the young. Some claim to have healing powers, as is detailed in Chapter Five.

One distinct feature of Islam in Senegal is the survival of many animistic beliefs and practices, which have been incorporated into religious observation. Often, people are uncertain of the origins of their traditions, confusing Islamic features with animist ones and vice versa. Thus, rather than conflicting, the two practices have meshed well in Senegalese society. Many self-defining Muslims believe very strongly in the power of fetishes, spirits, and *marabouts'* ability to alter the future.

PROSTITUTION IN SENEGAL

On August 28, 1969, the Senegalese initiated an interministerial effort to fight STDs. This was a direct response to increasing incidence and the moral implications of extramarital sex, held responsible for rapid and widespread transmission. The effort led to the creation of the National Bureau for the Battle against STDs (Bureau National de la Lutte Contre les MST) and the construction of several STD treatment centers in different regions of the country, including the STD clinic attended by the women in this study. To curtail activities leading to transmission, a law was passed in 1979 making it illegal for people under the age of twenty-one to practice prostitution. Offenders were sent to the town of Rufisque for imprisonment (Diop 1987).

Senegal's post-colonial legislation, however, was not the first government attempt to combat prostitution and control the spread of STDs, many informants told me. In 1960, just after French rule ended and the Senegalese began governing their own country, Prime Minister Maimed Dia, a "devout Muslim," became fed up with the "prostitution problem." He ordered all prostitutes to assemble in front of the public defender's office. He also advertised that all interested single men should go there as well. When the women arrived they were told to cover their faces with veils or bags. The men were then told to choose a bride without benefit of a conversation or glimpse of her face. This done, the minister instructed the men to pay their brides one hundred CFA (about ten cents). He then conducted a brief wedding ceremony, congratulated the thousands of newlyweds, and sent them home. This attempt to "save" women from prostitution actually succeeded in giving some women a helping hand out of the profession. In fact, some of the couples are still together.

While the minister's effort was a one-time event that went down in oral history, prostitution laws have consistently inhibited some women from entering the profession. But the numbers remain high. Today, experts estimate that six thousand prostitutes work in Dakar, approximately two-thirds of whom are registered at the clinic there (Mboup 1992). Diop (1987) estimates that twelve percent of the entire group are university students, while the majority of the rest are rural migrants. Kaolack has the second largest population of prostitutes, with an estimated 3,500 who are registered or clandestine. Ziguinchor, in the Casamance region, ranks third.

SOCIAL ISSUES AFFECTING THE LIVES
OF SENEGALESE WOMEN

The reality in Senegal is that women abandoned by men who once supported them frequently do not have any kind of support system, religious or otherwise. As a result, they have difficulty adjusting to single parenthood without the necessary training or education that would enable them to earn sufficient income. In the following pages I explore the issues that affect women, both prostitutes and non-prostitutes, in their daily lives and search for social acceptance and financial security. I have drawn on the literature and on the data acquired during observations and interviews with prostitutes and non-prostitutes.

MARITAL STATUS AND CHILDBIRTH

In Senegal, marriage is viewed as the joining of two forces in its uniting of two families. True love is rarely a consideration, while potential economic and social benefits frequently are. The cultural norm is still arranged marriage for young women, but the age at marriage has increased slightly (Pillsbury 1990). Marriages usually take place among members of the same caste and ethnic group, with occasional heterogeneous marriages meeting familial approval.

It is not uncommon for a man to be much older than his wife or wives. The gap in the age of spouses increases as the husband takes on additional, younger wives. Among the Serer, for example, the average age difference at marriage between a man and woman is 10.6 years for first wives, 15.9 for second wives, and 18.3 for third and fourth wives (Van de Walle 1990).

When a couple marries, they sign a contract indicating whether the marriage will be polygamous or monogamous. More than half the marriages in Senegal are polygamous (Gueye 1992), although every woman I spoke with preferred monogamy. Prior to the marriage, the man is required to pay a bride price, usually offered in the form of gifts and money at various stages during the courting period. Often, the woman and her family gives him a list of the objects she wants. Although the practice simulates the purchase of merchandise, Senegalese women see bride price as necessary security in the case of divorce or desertion (Heath 1988). At marriage the new bride usually moves into her husband's mother's compound or, increasingly in modern times, may start a new household with her husband and children, whom she is expected to conceive as soon as possible.

THE EDUCATION OF WOMEN

Traditionally, the Senegalese have educated fewer girls than boys, who are generally seen as needing more education to find jobs to support their wives and children. In rural areas, where many of the women in the study grew up, this still holds true because women's labor in the fields is essential for the production of subsistence and cash crops. In contrast, urban areas are characterized by a higher cost of living and scarce land. It is rare for an urban household to cultivate enough crops to support itself, and well-paying jobs are hard to come by.

Consequently, divorce among urban couples is often tragic for women, who are suddenly solely responsible for feeding and clothing their children in a large city far from relatives. Those who are not educated are doubly disadvantaged. Although some succeed at buying and selling goods, most do not have the capital needed to launch such an enterprise.

WOMEN AND WORK

Senegalese women, like many of their west African counterparts, are active traders of food, agricultural produce, and crafts. Most of the inhabitants in the region surrounding the town of Kaolack live in rural conditions where male and female household members contribute to agricultural production (Savane 1984). Fishing is also a source of subsistence and income (Nelson 1974). Livestock production, commerce, and handicrafts follow agriculture as the main sources of income, as there is little industry in Kaolack apart from a salt factory and a motorcycle and moped factory.

Women engaged in the informal sector in Kaolack are more likely to live in or near town, rather than in more remote villages. These women buy and sell produce, fish, prepared foods, crafts, and other goods. Kaolack women are known for their prominent role as cloth traders, bringing material from tax-free Gambia and selling it for substantially higher prices. Among those who have not been able to save the capital necessary to begin such endeavors or fail to keep them afloat, some are paid by wealthier households to clean house, cook, or do laundry. Others work in restaurants or factories in town.

HEALTH CARE IN SENEGAL

The Ministry of Health, located in Dakar, is responsible for health care throughout the country. At the regional level are *services de santé* (health departments); at the town level are *centres de santé* (health centers); at the local level in rural areas are *postes de santé* (health posts); and at the village level are *cases de santé* (health huts). The training level of staff and the quality and number of supplies decreases the further one travels from Dakar (Gueye 1992). In theory, the ministry supplies the regional services, which in turn supply those in town and so on, down to *cases de santé* .

Lack of equipment and medicine at all levels in all areas is the rule rather than the exception in African countries (Gueye 1992). Although limited supplies has always been a major concern, it is especially dire in the era of AIDS because it means that needles and other equipment that come into contact with blood are reused, often without the benefit of sterilization. Alcohol and equipment for boiling water are not consistently available at the lower levels of the system.

Six percent of Senegal's budget is spent on health care (Ndiaye et al. 1986). In Dakar, there is an average of one doctor per 23,000 people, while in smaller towns such as Louga, there is one doctor for every 162,000 (Ndiaye et al. 1986). The Kaolack region boasts one hospital, six *centres de santé*, forty-nine *postes de santé* in the city, and four hundred *cases de santé* in surrounding villages (FHI 1989). The services performed and populations served vary from location to location. For example, the Kaolack hospital treats wealthier urban residents and people who are seriously ill, and is the only location in the region where delivering women may receive caesarean sections.

AIDS IN SENEGAL

Although this book focuses on prostitutes and the issues affecting potential transmission between them and their sexual partners, it is necessary to note other ways in which HIV is spread within Senegal and between countries. Because of Senegal's location on the west coast of Africa and its continued role in international trade, it is a major commercial center and destination for people traveling to and from Europe and other African countries, who contribute to the spread of HIV throughout Senegal through sexual contact with locals. Many rural migrants travel to Dakar and may become infected in the capital, spreading the virus through sexual activity when they return to their homes (Mboup 1992; Kane and Mason 1993).

In 1986, six cases of AIDS were reported in Senegal. The number shot to 425 by 1991 (Viadro 1991). The figure as of 1992 was closer to 650 and the estimated number of HIV positive individuals was 51,000, or approximately two percent of the population (Mboup 1992). The most recent data indicate there were 1,297 people with AIDS in Senegal in 1994 (Global Programme on AIDS 1995). These statistics demonstrate that HIV rates were low in Senegal and that immediate and efficient efforts to stem its spread were crucial.

As part of the country's sentinel surveillance, the blood of prostitutes, hospital patients, men with severe STDs, pregnant women, and people with tuberculosis was tested regularly. The rates within these groups varied drastically from region to region. For example, HIV prevalence (this refers to HIV-1 and HIV-2 combined) among prostitutes was lowest in the northern regions of the country, such as Saint Louis (where, in 1989, 7.9 percent of prostitutes tested positive), increasing in Dakar (12.5 percent), Kaolack (30.3 percent), and Ziguinchor (46.2 percent), each further south than the previous location (Mboup 1992). Almost eleven percent of prostitutes tested nationally were HIV positive in 1991 (Ba 1991). In 1992, when this study was conducted, experts estimated that about forty percent of Kaolack prostitutes were HIV positive (Gueye 1992).

The number of seropositive men was also higher in Kaolack than elsewhere in the country. In 1991, the men in Kaolack who had severe STDs were tested for HIV; just over three percent were HIV positive. The rate of people with both tuberculosis and HIV infection in cities, however, was lowest in Kaolack at four percent, and highest in Dakar at almost six percent. The highest percentage of pregnant women testing positive was in Ziguinchor at three percent. Dakar's hospitals treated the most HIV positive individuals, who comprised almost sixteen percent of hospital patients in 1991 (Mboup 1992).

THE TWO VIRUSES: HIV-1 AND HIV-2

Senegal, like some of its west African neighbors, is faced with preventing the spread of two types of HIV, HIV-1 and HIV-2. Both forms of the virus suppress the body's immune system until the body cannot ward off infectious diseases, to which it eventually succumbs (Barabé et al, 1988).

HIV-1 is prevalent throughout the world and, among the Senegalese, is found primarily among individuals who have traveled outside of the country or have been in contact with those who have. The first two cases of HIV-1 infection in Senegal were discovered in 1985 (Barabé et al 1988). HIV-2 may have been present in Senegal as early as the mid-1960's, as the first infected individual was identified around 1970 through a Japanese survey in Senegal, Guinea, and the Ivory Coast. HIV-2 seems to be endemic to west Africa, occurring among individuals who have not left the western portion of the continent. Patients with HIV-2 tend to be older than those with HIV-1. This is partially due to the fact that people with HIV-2 seem to benefit from a longer latency period between infection and the onset of symptoms than do those with HIV-1. In addition, HIV-1 is eight to ten times more infectious per sexual act than is HIV-2 (Mboup 1992).

Until the second decade of AIDS, virtually all cases of HIV seropositivity in Kaolack and other locations outside of Dakar and Thies were HIV-2 (Mboup 1992). Recent statistics indicate that HIV-1 is spreading in Senegal, a fact that concerns researchers and doctors (Mboup 1992; Kane et al 1993).

Still, although researchers, clinic staff and others educated about HIV acknowledge the differences between the two viruses, prevention efforts generally do not separate the two. The primary reasons for this include the fact that the same behaviors lead to infection with HIV-1 and HIV-2 and the similar symptoms result from them, regardless of the time frame in which they occur. For these reasons, discussion of HIV prevention in this book does not differentiate between the two viruses prevalent in Senegal.

In setting the stage for exploring the impact of HIV on prostitute women in Senegal, this chapter has described the country's history, economy, religions and health care system with particular attention to their influence on women and their roles. As Farmer (1992) has shown, an understanding of a society's history and political economy is necessary to understanding the context of HIV transmission, prevention, and care. I now turn to a particular location in Senegal, Kaolack, and a point in time, 1991 and 1992, to examine the ways in which these factors have affected women today as they confront the challenges of sustaining their health and surviving economically.

2

Prostitution at the Crossroads

(There is a) need to understand how the macro level political economy af-
fects sociocultural dynamics at the micro level—including the spread of dis-
ease and the social response to epidemics.

(Schoepf 1992:280)

LIFE IN KAOLACK

Kaolack is located on the Saloum River, which feeds into the
Atlantic Ocean sixty miles west. Dakar, Senegal's capital and
the westernmost point of the African continent, is on the coast
one hundred and twenty miles northwest. In 1984 the town of
Kaolack had 127,000 residents, while the region surrounding it
had 1,200,000 (FHI 1989). Unlike Dakar, the "Paris of Africa";
Saint Louis, the "New Orleans of Senegal"; and Touba, the
country's "Mecca," Kaolack is not a town of particular history
or prestige. Mention Kaolack to a Senegalese and the standard

35

FIGURE 1

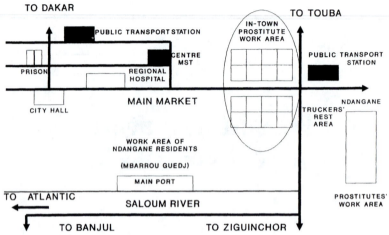

MAIN ROADS AND PLACES OF INTEREST

response is "it's too hot down there." In fact, Kaolack is most known for its heat, mosquitos, and peanut production.

Despite its negative reputation, most people traveling cross-country pass through the flat, dusty town. As one of the main intersections in Senegal, it is the junction of several national roads leading northwest to Dakar, northeast to Touba, southeast to Tambacounda, southwest to Banjul (the capital of the Gambia) and south through the Gambia to Ziguinchor. (See Figure 1 for a map of the area.) Kaolack is also accessible to many smaller cities and villages on and near the main roads. Consequently, it is frequented by rural dwellers selling crops and purchasing goods not available in small village markets. To accommodate travelers, the town boasts two public transport stations, a railroad station, a small airport, and an active river port.

As the capital of the region of Kaolack, the city has a governor, mayor, regional head doctor, regional hospital, regional

laboratory, fire station, police station, and a prison. It has two
large mosques and two outdoor markets that each cover several square blocks. Many Lebanese businessmen have migrated to the area, opening businesses such as a magazine and
paper store, a furniture store, an auto parts store, a grocery
store, and several small restaurants. In and around the down-
town area are several pharmacies and private health clinics
that serve the wealthier of Kaolack's residents. A dozen night
clubs and bars attract the younger crowd who congregate for
dancing and drinking in crowded, dimly lit rooms. These are
frequented by many of the in-town prostitutes, who, dressed
in their best *boubous*, share drinks and dance to loud American
and African music until finding a client, with whom they walk
to one of the inexpensive hotels nearby.

Just before the road leading south to Ziguinchor crosses
the Saloum River at the southern outskirts of town is the
neighborhood of Ndangane ("port" in the language of the
Serer). To the north of Ndangane is the heart of the city, bustling with street vendors, locals heading for the huge outdoor
market, and travelers on their way to or from the nearby transport station. This lively scene is contrasted to the area south of
Ndangane, a barren area marking the edge of town where the
shallow river stretches toward the ocean. It is in between the
transport station and the desert-like wasteland that the prostitutes of Ndangane—a group separate from the prostitutes
who work in town—work and live. The location is highly
symbolic of their place in Senegalese society.

Across the Ziguinchor-bound road from Ndangane is the
area of Mbaaru Geej (shelters by the sea). It is the work place
of the craftsmen, merchants, and fisherman whose families
settled at the town's port well before colonization. In the afternoon, old men gather under the many thatch shelters to rest,
talk, and drink tea. They wear wool caps despite the intense
heat and chew on *cure dents* as they listen to each others' stories. A fisherman, half the teeth missing from his crooked

smile, told me a story passed from generation to generation about the days when many Senegalese were taken as slaves to Europe and the Americas. During the peak of the slave trade the Senegalese emphasis on communal solidarity was invaluable; when someone would spot a large boat approaching the port, he would alert the others and everyone would run or row to a safe distance until the purpose of the visit was determined. Too many boys and men had been grabbed up and taken away, never to be seen again.

Because of the port's activity, shelters were built to shade the many laborers and vendors who flocked to the area hoping to make money. Huts were built for lodging and restaurants constructed to feed the many men who left their families behind in villages. One restaurant owner was a woman named Sala, the old fisherman said. Likely the first prostitute in Kaolack, Sala was known as Yayi Mbaar, mother of the shelters. Men knew they could take refuge at Sala's, enjoy a good meal, and retire to her back rooms to "rest." In those back rooms Sala would join each man in private. Eventually, Sala hired other women to accommodate her growing clientele.

When the old fisherman paused, my translator, a young intellectual, began to speak. "Prostitution was started by the colonialists," he asserted. "They took something that happened normally and commercialized it. They introduced currency and seduced our women into selling their bodies. What Sala did was beautiful and natural. What has happened since then is a sin."

The discussion under the shelters turned animated and lively, the men's voices cutting through the dense heat of the afternoon. "Women have always traded sex for economic support," one old man explained. "But today it has gotten out of hand." "Those women," another remarked as he leaned in the direction of Ndangane, "those women should beg in the streets instead of sinning. They won't go to the mosque when they die. No they won't."

Although the men nostalgically appreciate Sala's cooking and other services, they do not regard women who provide such services today with the same affection. During my conversations at Mbaaru Geej and with other Senegalese men, I found that this stigmatization of prostitution, coupled with open acknowledgment that men's participation perpetuates it, reflects the attitude of most Senegalese men. Although many married men would not hesitate to visit a prostitute, they do not think twice about criticizing prostitutes for engaging in sex outside of marriage—the sin of adultery. Ironically, none of the prostitutes in the study were married, but they estimated that half of their clients were. Still, while prostitutes are ostracized for their work, clients, who can more easily conceal their involvement, are exonerated (Caldwell et al. 1992). The men in Mbaaru Geej and their families have been trying relentlessly for three decades to drive the prostitutes from Ndangane. They have shown no affection—nostalgic or otherwise—for the women during their crusades against them.

PROSTITUTION IN KAOLACK

After our fruitful conversation with the men of Mbaaru Geej, my translator, Ibra, a scholar in public health and the history of prostitution, and I walked to a local gyros stand. We quenched our thirsts with *bissap*—a sweet, red punch made by boiling bitter red flowers with cups full of sugar—while he filled me in on the events and mainstream cultural values affecting the Kaolack prostitutes over the years. I asked about the meanings of words used to describe the prostitutes and their activities. He explained that well before the advent of AIDS and media claims that prostitutes were the vectors of the fatal virus, prostitutes were stigmatized in Senegal, as they are world-wide. In Senegal, the stigmatization of prostitutes and single women is expressed linguistically. The Wolof word *caga*, which originally referred to divorced or single women, is employed regularly in reference to prostitutes. Traditionally, the term described women "looking" for a husband. Looking involved going out with many men, and was accepted since it was a natural part of spouse selection.

Lacking a source of income while looking for a husband, many women asked male friends and acquaintances for money or gifts (Caldwell et al 1992; Little 1973). Ibra explained that as time went by people began to use *caga* in reference to women who were involved with several men who gave them money and material goods, whether the men were boyfriends or acquaintances associating with the women strictly for sexual relations. Eventually, the term was more commonly used to refer to women involved in the latter type of arrangement. It was adopted as the Wolof equivalent of the French *prostituée* (prostitute). *Cagatu*, therefore, is defined as the act of being a prostitute. However, Ibra said, the phrase *danga caga*, translated as "you have prostitute," means "you are attractive" and is used to compliment men and women.

Today, women react negatively to the word *caga* because it implies involvement in prostitution rather than divorce. Prostitutes do not use it to describe themselves. Instead, they speak of their work and colleagues in vague terms, referring to other prostitutes as "women who have cards." These cards show that they have registered as prostitutes with the police and STD clinic. When a woman does use *caga* in reference to a single female, she does so in either a joking or accusatory manner. When describing themselves, divorced women say *dama fasse* (I am divorced) rather than using *caga* in its original sense. Meanwhile, health practitioners are making efforts to find more neutral words to refer to prostitutes. The Wolof phrases *rafetu gudi* (beauty of the night) and *jigeen bu mbedd* (woman of the street) and their French counterparts (*belle de nuit* and *femme de la rue*, respectively) are increasingly common euphemisms.

Ibra explained that the stigmatization of prostitution is also apparent in the Senegalese people's outward treatment of women defined as *caga*. In the late 1950's, the prostitutes lived in Fangol, a residential area in Kaolack. When Fangol residents complained about the women, police began patrolling the area regularly. One night, an argument broke out between a client and a policeman. The dispute turned violent, and the client killed the policeman. The next morning, the police burned down the prostitutes' huts for revenge. Only the Diola palm wine salesmen, opted to stay and rebuild their makeshift bar. The prostitutes relocated to an uninhabited section of Ndangane. Known as the *syndicat*, the area earned its name as the location where craftsmen traditionally congregated to sell their wares. Because it was vacant at the time, the prostitutes reasoned that they too could sell their wares there.

The prostitutes built huts in the empty dirt lot bordering the paved road to the Gambia and agreed to pay rent to a Ndangane resident who said he owned the land. They also paid local homeowners for rented rooms in their housing compounds in the residential area separated from the *syndicat* by a wide dirt road. Together, the two areas are referred to as Ndangane.

The prostitutes' presence in the residential area has brought economic gain to their landlords as well as to the people who cook for them, do their laundry and sell them household goods, jewelry, and beauty products. These people are glad to have the women there. However, other residents, including the Serer fishermen and their families, have fought to have the prostitutes removed ever since their arrival. Through the years, these residents have set fire to the women's huts, beaten and kidnaped women, and summoned police assistance in attempts to scare the women away. In 1987, for example, several teenagers became angry with the lack of response to a letter they wrote to Senegal's president and set fire to the prostitutes' huts. The police arrived, showered the youth with tear gas, and imprisoned more than thirty of them for a month. The teens and their parents remain bitter because the prostitutes were defended rather than punished.

THE RIGHT TO PRACTICE

According to current Senegalese law, the prostitutes have the right to police protection. Although the primary purpose of the legislation was to decrease prostitution and the spread of STDs, women who register with the local police and a health care clinic and make semimonthly visits to the clinic are entitled to practice in peace. In fact, although the strict laws requiring registration have succeeded at discouraging some women from entering prostitution, they have also provided a significant service to the women who have registered. With the advent of AIDS in the early 1980s, Senegal's health clinics were in the ideal position to inform prostitutes about the virus, to test them for infection, and to encourage condom use by providing the women with free condoms. Also, drawing on the pre-existing structure, foreign researchers and donors have collected blood samples and monitored the prostitutes' health since 1987.

THE STD CLINIC'S AIDS PREVENTION EFFORTS

One clinic that responded quickly and efficiently to the threat of the pandemic is the STD clinic in Kaolack, founded in 1976. Given the town's location at the crossroads of the country, the high rate of HIV infection among the prostitutes there warranted drastic measures. Clinic staff recognized that efforts needed to be made to prevent transmission of the virus between various groups, including truck drivers, migrants, local clients, prostitutes, prostitutes' boyfriends, and partners of members of these groups.

When I arrived in Senegal the clinic was approaching the end of a two-year AIDS education campaign for its 258 registered prostitutes. The effort consisted of semimonthly presentations on AIDS and other health issues. The clinic staff led lectures and encouraged the prostitutes to discuss issues, ask questions, and request presentations on topics important to them. For convenience, these presentations were held after office hours in an old room in the clinic building. With small windows and broken fans, the room was suffocatingly hot when filled with seventy people, half of whom stood in the back due to a shortage of wooden benches. The staff showed video tapes on the few occasions that the tapes arrived on time from Dakar, the video machine was operable, and the only television was not in use elsewhere. During most meetings, however, the room was filled with lively discussion about coping with AIDS, caring for people living with AIDS, and dealing with neighbors who continually menaced the prostitutes. This open forum reflected the Senegalese emphasis on community and shifted some weight from the health care givers to the recipients, who had grown tired of having little say in their lives.

The safe sex messages imparted by clinic staff also appealed to the interests and sensitivities of the prostitutes. Information about AIDS prevention was couched in philosophical debates about the implications of spreading HIV to loved ones and unborn babies. The concept of sin—so significant in Senegalese life—was incorporated into discussions about the result of unsafe sex. A woman who knows about AIDS but exposes herself and others to the virus, repeated the staff over and over, is indirectly committing murder—an unpardonable sin.

These messages, coupled with the distribution of free condoms to prostitutes at the presentations and during their semimonthly examinations, made Kaolack's education campaign a potential model for other projects in the country. Not only did my interviews reveal the prostitutes' retention of AIDS knowledge and willingness to change their behavior

and risk losing valuable income by refusing unsafe sex, their
STD rates dropped substantially in the years following the
program's 1989 inception. In addition, their reported use of
condoms with clients doubled from forty-nine percent to over
ninety-eight percent. While it cannot be determined if the drop
in STD rates is directly attributable to the campaign or that
reported condom use necessarily reflects actual use, both findings have positive implications. The former indicates that exposure to STDs had declined for some reason, whether due to
decreased prevalence or due to increased protection. However, the fact that rates among non-prostitutes remained stable, according to clinic staff, increased protection seems a
likely contributor to the decrease. Even though the finding regarding increased condom use could not be verified short of
direct observation, it indicates, if nothing else, that the women
understood the messages conveyed by the clinic and knew
how to answer related questions. Knowledge is the first step,
though not the only step, required for behavior change.

But the added fact that the women reported less frequent
condom use with their boyfriends—reported use rose only
fourteen percent during the same time period—indicates the
women were not whitewashing their answers even though they
knew clinic staff hoped to hear their use had increased. For ob-
vious reasons, this finding was cause for concern because it
pointed to the need for interventions with boyfriends and a
breakdown in women's efforts to enforce safe sex behaviors.
The clinic staff responded to the discovery by meeting with boyfriends in neutral locations to educate them about AIDS and
condom use. Staff also focused on the issues during presentations for the prostitutes in hope of convincing them of the risks.
Staff held that the disparity in the rate of the women's condom
use with clients and boyfriends reflected the nature of relations
between prostitutes and their boyfriends, with whom they said
protected sex was not necessary because they were not strangers and could be trusted. Importantly, many of the women

feared their boyfriends would refuse to use condoms and would become angry with the women for implying the men might be infected with HIV or another STD. Thus, although the women intellectually understood the risks of unprotected sex with any man, including boyfriends, they were willing to take the chance with their boyfriends because they did not want to upset or lose them. They also wanted to believe their partners when they said they were healthy and faithful.

INTRODUCING THE *TOUBAB*

The day I arrived in Kaolack I attended one of the final AIDS presentations at the clinic. I felt small and intimidated when I peered into the room of Ndangane prostitutes, who looked nothing like the image one conjures of women in their profession. They were all shapes and sizes, with an average age of forty-six. No tight-fitting or revealing clothes for these matrons; they wore bright, multi-colored *boubous* and matching cloth wrapped around their heads and tucked over the top to cover their hair.

As I walked in, wearing a knee-length, pastel plaid cotton dress over a white tee shirt, I did not know where to sit. Should I sit up front on one of the few chairs reserved for clinic staff to establish myself as a staff member? Should I squeeze onto one of the wooden benches with the women to show I want to be seen as one of them? Or should I stand in the back to show that I do not want to be a distraction? The staff doctor motioned that I should take a seat near him. I pulled the chair toward the side wall to separate myself from the clinic staff and the prostitute audience so I could watch both simultaneously. Once seated, I instinctively propped my right ankle on my left knee, forming a triangle tented by plaid cloth. Used to wearing jeans, it took me a minute to realize the position did not work well in a dress. My female Senegalese friends in

Dakar had teased me for sitting in this distinctly American way. I quickly dropped my foot to the floor hoping nobody noticed. Exposing breasts is accepted, but exposing legs is not, nor is exposing the bottom of one's shoe, considered an insult in Muslim societies.

The doctor was silent as he waited for the rest of the staff to join him. I took a deep breath to compose myself. Being in that room seemingly in the middle of nowhere was one of those experiences that knocked me on the head and said "this is not a dream, you are here." Some of the women made eye contact with me and smiled before turning back to their friends. Others seemed not to notice me at all. Their gossip and laughter comforted me in its resemblance to family events and celebrations in which I would not take part for more than a year. Each time a woman walked through the door the room's occupants acknowledged her by saying her last name and asking how she was doing. "I am here only," each woman would respond— meaning that she is fine—as she squeezed onto a bench or walked to the back of the room to stand or lean against the wall.

Finally, three women and two men, all staff members, walked in and took their seats. The doctor tried to get the women's attention. When the conversation quieted to a low murmur he introduced me. His explanation of the *toubab*'s (white person's) presence was frequently interrupted as latecomers entered the room and the greeting ritual was reenacted; it would have been rude of the audience not to acknowledge each woman as she joined the meeting. In fits and starts the doctor explained that I had come to conduct research on the influence of AIDS on their lives, that I would be a staff member for ten months, and that they were to give me their full cooperation throughout my stay.

"She is a friend of Mary Lee's," he said poignantly, and the audience nodded and whispered in understanding. Mary was the American medical student who conducted interviews with the women two years earlier at the beginning of the AIDS education campaign (Lee 1989). Although Mary and I had spoken only once by telephone, connecting my name to that of someone the staff and prostitutes already knew and trusted helped subside concern about my presence and credibility. Fanning myself with my note pad as the doctor continued, Mary's words of advice echoed in my head. "If I were you I'd go somewhere else. Have you been there at the peak of the dry season?"

It was too late to go elsewhere and I felt confident that I was meant to be in Kaolack with this group of women. The country's leading AIDS researcher had advised me to go there to document the "culture of prostitution" and to evaluate the effectiveness of the AIDS education campaign targeted at this group of at-risk women, my study was well-defined, the findings would be useful in-country, and I would be working closely with women. All these factors were important to me and outweighed the negative reactions of people who had spent time in the Kaolack heat.

When I drifted back to the conversation, the women were raising a pressing question: "What is her Senegalese name?" I said that I did not have one, although my Dakar friends had suggested a few. Someone shouted "Coumba!" and everyone agreed. I liked the sound of it. Then came the more important question: "What will her last name be?" From the packed room came shouts of common Senegalese last names, each woman suggesting a different one. Knowing that names were tied to ethnicity and about choosing one over the others, I chose Sow, Uncle Ibrahima's last name.

Ibrahima Sow is a prominent agricultural researcher in Kaolack who, in adopting me as his "niece," found me a house, helped me order furniture, and let me stay with his family for the first few nights while my house was being painted. In the meantime, he sent a messenger to the countryside, telling one of his former house guards, Mbodj, to report to Kaolack the following day to guard my house. Ibrahima and the clinic staff insisted that, as a single white woman, I

should have a 24-hour guard to protect me and my belongings. Although there did not seem to be imminent danger, this
was a precaution taken by most foreigners and wealthy
Senegalese to discourage potential thieves. Ibrahima also
spoke to a friend of his who lived around the corner from my
house and, without my knowledge, asked if his daughter,
Youma, would be my friend and Wolof tutor. When she offered to be my tutor I was surprised and excited.

Such hospitality stemmed from the fact that I was an
acquaintance of Ibrahima's niece. She was engaged to an
American acquaintance of mine, who asked if I would accom-
pany her to the U.S. embassy, where she was having trouble
getting a visa to move to the United States. I had just begun
dating Michael, who worked at the embassy, and asked if he
would ask the consulate about the status of my friend's visa.
Her visa arrived a few days later and within weeks she was
reunited with her fiance. Connections are everything, I
thought.

"Sow?!" the women laughed and cheered. With that name I
became a Peulh, or Fulbe, an ethnic group known for cattle
raising, selling dairy products, and, unbeknownst to me, their
supposed proclivity to prostitution.

When the meeting ended several women shook my hand as
they left the conference room. In hesitant Wolof I told them I
was glad to be there. I helped them straighten the room then
said goodbye. I walked outside into the courtyard surrounded
by decrepit, off-white buildings housing the dispensary's
many offices. I leaned against my car and watched the women
disperse. While some piled into taxis, others walked down the
dirt road to one of the town's few paved roads, perhaps to
hitch a ride or catch a bus. They would all eventually reunite
in Ndangane, where they would gather to discuss what they
learned at the presentation and how it affected them.

I looked at the dispensary and wondered how healing could
take place within its walls. The paint was peeling, the floors

were stained, the electricity failed regularly, and the only tech-
nological equipment available was that provided by Harvard
University for the STD clinic's AIDS research activities. There
were always more patients than could be seen on a given day,
some of whom would never be seen because they could not
afford the twenty-five cent entrance fee. Wealthier patients
were more likely to go to the only regional hospital or one of
several private clinics, where they would get better care and
more personal attention for a higher fee.

Next to the STD clinic was the dentist's office. To the right
was the family planning clinic, and beyond that the public latrine: two stalls with holes in the cement floor and a hanging
knob that occasionally responded to a pull by flushing water
into the holes. Across from the latrine was the pharmacy. Patients stood in line outside waiting their turn to talk to the
pharmacist through a hole in the wall. Catty-corner from him
was the general clinic, where adults waited on uncomfortable
wooden benches to see a general practitioner. One of the clinic's three practitioners was also the director of the dispensary.
He lived in one of the rooms upstairs, next to the dispensary
janitor and his wife. I looked up from the courtyard and saw
the doctor, who was observing activities from his balcony
while talking to someone on his cordless phone. I did a dou-
ble-take; it struck me that such high-tech equipment could be
found amid such poverty.

To the left of the director's office was the pediatric and vac-
cination clinic, from which rang children's cries of pain as they
were given injections. Not far from there was the adult in-
patient room, quiet and dark, with its half-dozen beds occupied. At the end of the hall was the maternity ward, where the
mothers were quiet and the babies loud. Hearing a baby cry, I
walked over, eager to see new life. He was extremely small
and light brown. His mother held him, looking content but
not particularly happy. Her labor had been short and, like a
courageous Senegalese woman, she had not shown her pain

despite the lack of anesthesia. She would stay there with him
that night then return to her village the next day because she
and her son appeared healthy. In a few days she would
resume her work in the fields.

The small, windowless room's walls were eggshell white,
peeling and stained with spatters of blood and other body fluids. One bare light bulb hung from the ceiling. The new
mother lay on a bare metal table. There was blood underneath
her, and a trail of red leading from the table to the counter
where the just-used forceps awaited cleaning. Two other forceps were ready for the quiet women lying on tables flanking
the new mother. The instruments, which were the only instruments in the room, soaked in cold water. Three forceps for
three tables, while other women in the first stages of labor
waited their turn in an adjoining room. If the babies needed to
be delivered before the tables were vacant, a nurse's assistant
would start delivery in the waiting room, running to the delivery room to grab a forceps if one was available. If one was
not, she would go without. Going without is a common activity in Senegalese life, and it accounts for people's amazing re-
silience and resourcefulness.

I walked back to the STD clinic and ran into the doctor on
his way out. He was several inches over six-feet tall, with a
quick smile, deep voice, and crossed-eyes. Trying not to look
distracted, I wondered how this affected his vision and spatial
perception. He asked if I wanted to join him for dinner. I accepted, reminding him that I am a vegetarian and did not
want to inconvenience or insult him. He said there would be
plenty of vegetables in the *mafe* his cook was preparing. Since
most Senegalese dishes were made with fish or beef, I was
growing used to picking around the meat and ignoring the
fact that the sauce contained animal juices. In fact, I was at the
point where I often craved *mafe*, with its peanut sauce, carrots,
manioc, potatoes, miniature green pumpkins, and chunks of
beef poured over short-grained rice.

I knew my way along the dirt roads to his apartment because I had visited on earlier trips from Dakar. The second-floor apartment was comfortable, with two bedrooms, a kitchen, and a common area with a glass dining table and mattresses on the floor for lounging. They were also used for sleeping when the apartment was crowded with the doctor's many boyhood friends who grew up in his village outside Kaolack. The only drawback was the constant buzz of flies and mosquitos that entered the room through holes in the window screens. They swarmed inside at meal time, drawn by the scent of food and humans.

Two of his boyhood friends, who had been staying with him "temporarily" for more than a year, joined us at the table. Three of us ate out of the communal bowl with spoons. The fourth used his hand to make balls of rice, which he popped into his mouth with impressive ease. I had not yet mastered the art of making rice balls single-handed, and did not want to practice in front of them. The men helped me out by taking beef from my quarter of the bowl and substituting it with vegetables from theirs. When I felt full, I put down my spoon. They were surprised that I ate so little. I said that the food was very good, but I had eaten enough. They told me that I was too thin, insisting I should eat more so I would look like a Senegalese woman, large and shapely. I was beginning to like this place.

The men finished the contents of the bowl, my section included, and sat back to relax. The cook brought out a teapot and four shot glasses. The doctor went through the ritual of mixing several cubes of sugar with the brewed tea, pouring it skillfully from a foot above each glass, and passing liquid from glass to glass until each was full, capped by an inch of foam. The men lifted their glasses and drank the entire contents in a few successive gulps. The tea was too hot for me, so I sipped it. Seeing that the cook was waiting for me to finish so she could start the second round, I drank it quickly, hoping no one noticed me wince. She then brought the second round, which was sweeter and mellower than the first. The doctor had just poured the third and sweetest when someone knocked on the door.

It was the dispensary janitor, who had come to announce that one of the doctor's patients was ready to give birth. Normally the obstetrician would have overseen the delivery herself, but the patient was suspected of being HIV infected and it was the doctor's responsibility to take a blood sample from the umbilical cord and sterilize the forceps after use. They were taking these unusual precautions because the doctor had recently treated the woman's husband for apparent AIDS-related symptoms, but still did not know his status because the test results had not arrived.

I asked the doctor if I could join him and he agreed, swigging down what remained of his tea. He asked the janitor if he had the keys for the STD clinic laboratory, where the dispensary's only sterilizing oven was located. The janitor said he had given the spare to the lab technician, who lost his set. The doctor and I drove to the technician's house to fetch the keys while the janitor returned to the clinic. The technician's wife greeted us and said her husband was in the neighborhood performing a circumcision. He was not trained, but had taught himself the procedure so he could make more money. I already knew of his activities because Maria, the nurse who translated for me during interviews, had illustrated the technician's various money-making schemes by grasping invisible money from the air and putting it into imaginary pockets. She clearly disliked him, as did the prostitutes, I would find out later. His wife offered us tea while their daughter went to find the technician. We declined graciously, explaining we had just finished. We sat in bamboo chairs in the shade of the cement courtyard and waited. Their three-year old daughter emerged from one of the stucco rooms and walked up to me slowly. I held my hand out to her. She touched it with a finger then jumped back, expecting something to happen. When nothing did, she touched me again. I took out my note pad and drew a cat. She identified it in Wolof, and I learned a new word. I drew a happy face and she smiled.

The technician arrived with an air of importance, impromptu medicine kit in hand. The doctor explained the situation and the technician said he was ready to go. I wondered why he could not just hand the keys to the doctor, but did not ask. Much later I learned the importance of responsibility and control to staff members; the laboratory was his domain, so he wanted to be there, even if only to turn the key. We drove to the clinic and I parked in front of the maternity ward. The technician went to prepare the lab, while the doctor and I went into the delivery room. Only the middle metal table was occupied. It was the STD patient—a young, attractive woman who was so small that in another setting I would have not guessed her pregnant. The doctor shook her hand and I greeted her from a distance. Because she did not appear to be having contractions, I walked outside to get some air.

Only a few minutes passed before I heard the baby cry. I was amazed at how quickly the small woman had given birth and walked in to see for myself. The obstetrician held the baby boy while the clinic doctor, who had donned rubber gloves, inserted a needle into the umbilical cord. It took several tries before he was able to get enough blood. I started feeling a bit queasy, but the mother and baby were too tired to be bothered by the doctor's activities.

The doctor thanked the obstetrician and promised to return the needle and forceps within an hour. He took them and the blood-filled test tube to the laboratory and gave them to the technician, who labeled the blood and stored it in the refrigerator until he could find a way to transport it and dozens of accumulated samples to Dakar for testing. He then put the needle and forceps into the oven and set the timer for an hour. I remarked that it was lucky the forceps would not be needed soon. Both men agreed, but they had accepted the limitations in their country and no longer worried themselves with what-ifs.

I looked around the laboratory, a small room divided down the middle by a white tile counter. The walls, like those inside most Senegalese buildings and homes, were sky blue, decorated with posters illustrating the ways in which AIDS is transmitted. Two large, graphic photographs of men's and women's genitalia infected with STDs hung at eye level. I looked away and took note of the donated equipment: two microscopes, two sinks, a large refrigerator, a large sterilizing oven, and a small sterilizer. In the many cupboards were test tubes and disposable needles, all sent for AIDS surveillance activities.

After forty minutes, when the technician and doctor decided the oven contents were sufficiently sterilized, the technician removed the contents with a hot pad. He took them to the obstetrician then met the doctor and me at my car. I dropped off the doctor at his apartment, then drove the technician to a house where he was scheduled for another circumcision. He asked if I could wait to give him a ride home. I said I could not. I drove home to Uncle Ibrahima's, where I drank *bissap* and watched a soccer game with him and his three sons. His wife, a nurse at a family planning clinic, and their two daughters were rarely in the common family room when I visited. When the game was over I walked outside and down the stairs to the guest room. I waited for the night guard to finish in the bathroom, then washed up. I went into my sky blue room, locked the door, sprayed for mosquitos, turned on the air conditioner, and wrote in my journal until I fell asleep. The two-inch foam mattress and low, wooden bed was surprisingly comfortable, although I always stumbled getting up in the morning, forgetting how close I was to the concrete floor.

I moved into my new house on a Friday, so Michael drove the nearly three hours from Dakar to spend my first night there with me. The electricity would not be turned on for a few days, but I wanted to unpack and get settled before I started full-time fieldwork that Monday. Michael brought candles, mosquito repellent, cheese, fruit, peanut butter, and

French bread. We picnicked on my relatively thick foam mattress—the only furniture in the house—and listened to the sounds of Senegal: drums, donkeys, goats, social gatherings, and Mbodj's footsteps as he patrolled the yard.

On Saturday we drove around town picking up supplies and scouting for places of interest. Anxious for a sense of privacy and some protection from the sun, I bought material at the market place and took it to Ibrahima's tailor to be made into curtains. On the way, we drove by the clinic so Michael could see my new place of work. His first thought was that the dispensary buildings were abandoned. The janitor let us into the offices, and their sparseness and age did little to change Michael's first impression. It was then that I realized that after only a few days in Kaolack I was noticing such details less and less.

STRUCTURE AND FUNCTION OF THE STD CLINIC

On Monday morning I waited excitedly for the social worker to arrive at the clinic. He had promised to explain his filing system to me so I could begin going through the prostitutes' records to learn about them and decide how to choose a study sample from the registration roster. During the following months I gathered information about the women and Senegalese culture by examining the women's files, conducting formal interviews with the women, and having informal conversations with clinic staff and male and female friends. In all, I interviewed sixty-eight prostitutes and thirty-two non-prostitutes from the beginning of September through mid-October.

To gain an understanding of the culture of the clinic, I analyzed the clinic's structure and function, including the staff duties and relationships with the prostitutes who visited for semimonthly health examinations and with *externes* (the staff's term for men and non-prostitute women who visit the clinic for STD diagnosis and treatment because they are external to the program). The STD clinic had one doctor, one head nurse, one nurse, one nurse's aide, one social worker, and one laboratory technician. The technician had an assistant who was paid with the money the dispensary charged each patient for diagnosis and treatment.

The head nurse, nurse, and nurse's aide examined all female STD patients and pregnant women with health problems. The nurse listed the names and conditions of the prostitutes in a record book and wrote comments about the women's health in their files. She also entered the names and ages of *externes* in the record book, while the head nurse wrote monthly reports documenting the number and nature of the STDs they treated. When an *externe* tested positive for an STD the doctor or head nurse counseled him or her about the illness and the danger of unprotected sex, explaining the threat of AIDS. Each patient was encouraged to bring in his or her partner for STD testing and treatment to avoid reinfection.

The doctor examined patients with very serious or unique illnesses. He also interviewed newly registered prostitutes to gather demographic and health information, which he recorded on questionnaires provided by Harvard University. The staff were supposed to update these questionnaires every six months when they drew the prostitutes' blood for surveillance of seroprevalence rates, but many of the records were incomplete.

The social worker kept track of the women's files and was responsible for counseling them when they had social problems. When new prostitutes registered, he discussed their decision with them and started their files. He and the doctor had recently begun to introduce the topic of AIDS to women signing up for the first time. They also asked each woman to sign a form giving consent for AIDS testing.

The laboratory technician tested all genital cultures, saliva, and blood for illnesses other than HIV. He extracted cultures from the men, while the nurses were responsible for the

women. The nurses also took blood from registered prostitutes during their thorough examinations every six months,
from STD patients with severe STDs, and from patients referred by other doctors who suspected HIV infection. The
technician sent the blood to Dakar for HIV testing. Dakar
clinic staff then sent select blood samples to Harvard University and the World Health Organization (WHO) within a few
weeks. The results of the prostitutes' tests were usually sent to
Kaolack after a few months, while those of other STD patients
seldom made it to Kaolack unless staff made several requests.

Each prostitute was expected to visit the clinic every two
weeks for a short visit, during which a nurse inserted a
speculum into the woman's vagina to look for symptoms of
STDs. Such visits took place every day of the week. If the
nurse saw nothing abnormal, she gave her patient twenty-
eight free condoms and told her she was free to go. If the nurse
suspected an illness, she took a culture and sent it to the laboratory while the prostitute waited for her test results. If the
prostitute tested positive for an STD, the nurse held her registration card and gave her a prescription. If the medication
were available at the clinic, the nurse would give it to the prostitute for free. If the medication were a gift that the nurse received from a medicine salesman, she might ask the prostitute
for some money in return. If the medication were not available at the clinic, the woman could request it for free at the
dispensary pharmacy. If not in supply there, the woman
would have to go to a pharmacy in town, where it was very
expensive. She could not practice prostitution legally while
waiting for the medication to cure the STD. After four or five
days she would be tested again, receiving her registration card
only if cured.

When menstruating, prostitutes left their registration cards
at the clinic. This was difficult for them because it meant they
would not make any money until cured. However, clinic staff
emphasized the importance of this rule in the era of AIDS,

especially because the presence of blood increases chances of HIV infection during sexual intercourse.

Every forty-five days the prostitutes' visits were long visits, which required that they undergo a physical examination and have laboratory tests done. These took place only on Mondays, Wednesdays, and Fridays. The women arrived around nine or ten o'clock in the morning and did not get their laboratory test results until three or four. If their results were negative they were given their registration cards and free condoms. If their results were positive they could not have their cards, but were given a prescription to cure their STDs.

The wait for test results was long because the laboratory technician and his assistant took lunch breaks from one o'clock to two-thirty regardless of the workload. The women usually waited in the large room used for presentations or went into town for a few hours. Some clinic staff went home to eat, but most of them ate together in the main office. The head nurse's family usually sent over a large bowl of *ceebu jen* (rice and fish) and the staff pulled chairs around the communal bowl, propped on a chair, and ate with their hands or large spoons.

Understanding the relationship between clinic staff and the two groups of registered prostitutes (those who worked in town and those who worked in Ndangane) was crucial to understanding the context in which the prostitutes reacted to the threat of AIDS in their daily lives. The most striking feature of their interactions was the staff's ability to be simultaneously supportive and critical of the prostitutes, who appreciated the assistance but strongly resented the long waits and perceived mistreatment by staff, some of whom they described as judgmental and controlling. Similarly, understanding the distinct economic, social, and psychological factors affecting the two groups of prostitutes was salient in understanding the issues surrounding the women's attitudes, behavior, and perception of their work, themselves, and their place in society. The dynamics of the prostitutes' daily lives are described in the chapters to follow, in which I focus on life for Ndangane prostitutes while reflecting on episodes from my daily life in their neighborhood, encounters with clinic staff, and conversations with prostitutes who worked in town.

3

Taking Charge

Some of the women drink the money they earn. I take charge of mine.
—Fatou

After a month of watching drama in the STD clinic, the big breakthrough in my relationship with the Ndangane prostitutes came one afternoon when I offered several women a ride home after they were given their STD test results. Cars are a luxury in Senegal, and none of the prostitutes owned one. I bought mine in Dakar when I learned I would be living several miles from the clinic. I also wanted the freedom to drive to Dakar.

By driving the women home I saved them cabfare and took a step into their world. The first time I drove seven of them home in my five-seater, I dropped them off on the dirt road that separated the residential area from their work area. The second time, I stayed for a chat. The third time, they took me for a tour of their work huts. By my fourth visit, I no longer needed an excuse to visit. I just parked on the side of the dirt road and walked from hut to hut to greet the women, who

FIGURE 2

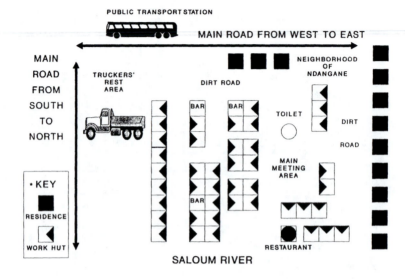

were slowly becoming my friends. (See Figure 2 for a map of the work area).

TAKING ACTION

During my progressively frequent visits to Ndangane, I became aware of the roles the women played within their community. Women like Rhama and Fatou took charge of their lives and took care of the women who had "abandoned" themselves by drinking, letting their health slip, and "wasting" money that could have been spent on food, condoms, and their families. Those who took charge loaned the others money and bought large quantities of condoms from family planning centers and pharmacies when supplies at the clinic were low. Their willingness to spend money for their own and others' protection was significant in a cultural setting where money was very scarce and most would have put their fate in the hands of God rather than take cash from their purses to ward off an invisible virus.

Of the dozen or so women who were most active in making decisions about group welfare in Ndangane and at the clinic, four were chosen as delegates to present communal concerns to clinic staff, the police department, the Regional Medical Officer, the press, and any visitors they might receive. Rhama was one of the delegates, elected because of her fluency in French, adequate writing skills, and willingness to subtly ruffle feathers to gain respect and condoms. She bought boxes of condoms more often than her colleagues did and freely doled them out while keeping tabs on who owed her. Her friends paid her back in kind as soon as they could, knowing she would gently but constantly remind them of their debt.

NDEYE

Another delegate was Ndeye, a strong-willed woman who did not own a hut in the prostitute's work place. Instead, she worked out of the compound she shared with her boyfriend of ten years, Ibou, and their two children. Ibou was the leader of an informal association of *concubins* (men who live with prostitutes). Still, the family lived within shouting distance of the work huts, and Ibou—a large, strong man who towered over the petite, feminine Ndeye—was often summoned to defend threatened prostitutes. He was also responsible for conveying the men's concerns to clinic staff. In response to his recommendation, clinic staff staged informal AIDS information sessions in Ndangane for men who needed education but would never visit the STD clinic.

Like Ibou, Ndeye was determined and motivated to improve her situation. They both stayed in regular contact with Ibra, the influential social worker who left the clinic following a dispute with the staff. Ndeye and the other women still grieved over his departure because he was a devoted advocate of their rights and interests. The remaining social worker never visited Ndangane for fear that someone would mistake him for a client and the word would get back to his wife. A former nurse, he was more likely to close his office doors to examine an ailing relative than to let the prostitutes confide to him their many social, psychological, and financial problems.

Angry that the prostitutes had lost a valuable ally and service, Ndeye continued to inform Ibra of the women's problems. He always reacted immediately and compassionately. He occasionally asked me to join him and one of the delegates on visits to the Chief of Police and the Regional Medical Officer to speak on the women's behalf. I completed the team: a professional, educated man; an articulate prostitute; and a *toubab* with a car. "It always helps to have a *toubab* along," he said. "The leaders are more likely to listen."

I never actually spoke much in these situations, but it did seem my presence caught people's attention. I joked about being the token white, but I did not mind being "used" for the women's benefit. As Rabinow has pointed out (1977), ethnographic fieldwork is a give-and-take situation. The anthropologist uses informants for information, and, in most cases, informants will be more cooperative if they are able to use the anthropologist to obtain something in return for their valuable knowledge and insight. Thus, an effective way to gain entree is to offer services otherwise unattainable by informants. As I did, Rabinow used his car to gain access and information. Requests for rides, however, became so overwhelming that he was relieved when his car broke down. In my situation, the prostitutes were extremely considerate, rarely asking for rides, but always accepting when I offered. Certain members of the clinic staff, on the other hand, made me uncomfortable with their requests for rides, money, and other favors. I found myself slowly withdrawing from their company once my study of the clinic was completed, preferring instead to spend my time with the prostitutes in Ndangane.

SADIO

The visits I made with Ibra and the delegates were a welcome diversion, giving me the opportunity to see how changes, albeit very small ones, were made to improve the prostitutes' lives. The delegate who accompanied Ibra most often was Sadio, a small woman with high cheek bones and eyes that crinkled when she smiled. She usually jumped at the opportunity to put on her nicest *boubou* and drive around town with us. High-strung and more secretive than the other women, Sadio was surprisingly open about her fear of AIDS. Perhaps because she was the first woman I interviewed, she became very concerned that my choosing her as an informant meant she was HIV positive. In truth, she was, but neither she nor the other women would learn of their status for several months. Maria explained to Sadio that we were interviewing every woman who entered the clinic's door and that Sadio just happened to be the first. Unconvinced, she repeated that she was very worried. "How would I tell my children?" she asked. "My children are my life."

Sadio was born in 1954. Although she wanted to go to school, her father did not see the need for educating a female, and chose a husband for her when she was fifteen years old. After as many years of marriage, she divorced the first husband, married a second, then divorced again. When her father died Sadio used the family's insurance money to move her four children and her mother to Dakar. Once settled, she sold fish for four months, but only made thirty cents a day.

Hearing that the most popular prostitutes in Kaolack could make upwards of four dollars a day, Sadio left her family and headed south for her new profession. She eventually met a man and moved in with him. He was extremely temperamental but she endured his beatings, thinking she had little choice. One day, clinic staff announced during a presentation that the clinic would assist women subjected to domestic abuse. She told them of her situation, and within days her boyfriend was in jail. But Sadio felt sorry for him, so she took him food every day until he was released. Reading her kindness as forgiveness, he went straight to their compound the day he was set free. Much to his dismay, Sadio was gone and his belongings were neatly stacked in front of the locked door.

Worried about infection and tired from the worry, Sadio worked hard to bring about small changes in her community of women. Yet when I asked what she would do if she could do anything in the world, she answered, "I cannot do much because I am so tired. I am tired only." Being tired in Ndangane involved much more than a physical need for sleep. Sadio and others explained that they were tired of prostituting themselves, tired of worrying about AIDS, tired of warding off violent clients, and tired of praying for assistance and not receiving it.

Still, Sadio worked up the energy to visit the local leaders and saw it as her way of fighting for the rights of women who often described themselves as powerless. When we visited the officials, she was content to remain wordless at Ibra's implicit insistence. Clearly, he was the designated speaker and we the silent representatives. Visibly proud of his rapport with these authority figures, Ibra always displayed respect and graciousness in their presence. Through example, he demonstrated the importance of working within the hierarchy, which included taking high profile out-of-town visitors by the police station and the region's medical office before taking them anywhere else. For the same reasons, Mbodj always took Michael and me to see the village chief when we visited his village. We would shake the chief's hand, sit on the edge of a bed in his dark hut while he and Mbodj greeted each other, then be on our way. Judging from Mbodj's big smile, this small gesture meant a great deal.

COUNA

Through analysis of the women's social activities in Ndangane I learned that elders, like village leaders, had earned—and expected—to be treated with respect. Older prostitutes were in a precarious situation, however. They had finally reached the age at which women were theoretically accorded the same respect as men, yet they were in a profession that affords them no prestige or social role outside the bounds of their tight-knit community. Couna, a fifty- something dynamo, struggled with the conflict and disappointment of passing the benchmark of menopause with little public acknowledgment of her new status. Yet among the prostitutes, she was a leader and an elected delegate. Though small and grandmotherly in appearance, she was an excellent public speaker who gained the respect of clinic staff through her persistence and congeniality. Such respect was not granted lightly by staff, who, despite their sympathy for the women, regarded them as sinners because of their sexual activity.

Watching Couna in action, I was reminded of politicians filibustering on the senate floor. She would not sit down until she was convinced she had made her point by talking long enough to make her opponents forget their argument. Her silent colleagues appreciated her outspoken manner at the clinic's semimonthly presentations. Couna said what many of them hesitated to say, lest they be criticized by clinic staff. But their agreement with her was clear; when she spoke, her declarations were followed by affirming "mmm"s, nodding, and tongue-clicking reminiscent of supportive "amen"s during a Southern Baptist church service.

During my visits, Couna and the other prostitutes enforced her role in their fictive family. They told me that I should always pass by Couna's hut to shake her hand and greet her. I learned that greeting is not only an integral part of every encounter in Senegal, but that it is also a means for demonstrating respect to elders. The more respect an individual deserves, the more embellished the exchange. Repeating the person's last name is also an affirmation of her importance. Although I knew this, I sometimes avoided saying Couna's last name because I had difficulty pronouncing so many vowel sounds in succession. Without fail, she prompted me each time by saying her name, as if I had forgotten it. I would repeat it, she would then say my last name, I would say hers again, and so on until she initiated a conversation.

When I had questions about other cultural "rules," a few people helped me understand their purpose and symbolism. My three key informants were Mbodj; Youma, my neighbor and Wolof tutor; and Khady, one of the leaders in Ndangane. Whereas Mbodj and Youma often spoke with me during the evening, Khady spent many day-time hours with me in Ndangane and around town, philosophizing about her work, religion, money, and men.

KHADY

Khady was a heavy, light-skinned woman in her thirties. She had wide-set eyes and a pleasant, gap-toothed smile. She was very animated, speaking as much with her hands and body as with words, and capable of a laugh that would resonate across the huts of Ndangane. On my first solo visit to Ndangane she beckoned me into her hut and, in excellent French, told me she was scared of AIDS. Most nights she stayed up worrying about infection and illness. I explained that she was doing the right thing by making her clients wear condoms and visiting the clinic regularly to monitor her health. "But my boyfriend won't wear condoms, and I would lose him if I insisted." Did he see other women? Probably. This was a common complaint among the prostitutes. "And in Mauritania we knew nothing of condoms, Coumba. And we had many, many clients."

Long before they worked in Kaolack, Khady, Rhama, and several other Ndangane prostitutes lived in Mauritania, the

Muslim state north of Senegal. The women had heard that
prostitutes could live more peacefully and extravagantly
there, so women who had worked together in Dakar were
reunited in Mauritania in the mid 1980's. They arrived under
different circumstances, but for the same purpose: to practice
prostitution where the cost of living was low and police intru-
sion was minimal. The women made more money per client
than in Senegal and worked out of their own homes, a luxury.
Because prostitution was illegal in Mauritania, however, there
were no clinics prepared to monitor their health or to give
them condoms and information about STDs and AIDS.

Unaware of the growing health risks in the years after HIV
was first identified, the women enjoyed their new home.
Many bought houses and took advantage of the low cost of
cloth and other consumer goods. Periodically, they took goods
home to Dakar for their mothers and sisters to sell for profit.
Some of the women even married and began to feel that their
previously tumultuous lives were finally settling down.

In 1989, however, age-old Senegalese-Mauritanian border
disputes escalated, and all Senegalese were forced out of the
country and flown back to Senegal. The women took all the
possessions they could carry to the airport, only to have them
confiscated by authorities before they boarded the plane. Khady
returned to her family with her third husband, whom she had
married in Mauritania. After hearing that this man had lost a
business and had no way to support Khady and their baby girl,
Khady's father told her to leave her husband. He had given his
daughter equally strict orders throughout her life. But Khady
disobeyed him, as was her habit when his demands did not
seem in her best interests. Her independent thinking had
caused conflicts between the two for most of her life.

When Khady was seven, her father retired and took her out
of school, saying he could no longer afford to send her. He sent
her to live with an aunt who used her as a maid. At fourteen
Khady moved back home and her father insisted she marry a
friend his age. She resisted, as did her mother and other family

members who tried to convince him it was a bad idea. Ignoring them, her father saw to it that the couple was married. A few months after the wedding, Khady ran away and took up with a young man from Togo, who supported her while she looked for work. Eventually, a family member spotted her at the open-air market and told her father. He sent Khady's older sister to find and retrieve her. Reluctantly, Khady returned. As she approached her father to greet him, he grabbed her, quickly tying her hands and feet. "I could barely feed myself. And he cut off all of my hair," she recalled, unconsciously running her hand through her thin, long braids. For a month he ignored his wife's pleas to untie Khady. The day he finally set her free, Khady left the house to fetch water and disappeared for several months.

The second time Khady was found and taken home by a relative, her father consented to her divorce from "the old man with rough hands and bad breath." He also agreed she could marry a relative she had liked since childhood. The marriage, however, could not take place until Khady repaid her first husband the bride price he gave her family when they married. As was customary, her mother's brother paid the debt.

Khady and her second husband lived with her parents. Thankful for her divorce and new marriage, she set out to find work. During her fruitless search she ran into an old friend who had become a prostitute. Dressed in fancy clothes and wearing flashy jewelry unknown to girls from small villages, the friend convinced Khady to try prostitution, stressing that she would attract many clients because of her large size. The friends decided Khady should tell her family that she had landed a job in a fish-drying factory in nearby Dakar. The next morning, Khady left home early to keep up the facade. She bided her time in town, went home for dinner, then devised an excuse to go out again. Her real work day began after dark when the bars in town opened. Well after midnight she walked home, snuck quietly into her hut, and slept for a few hours, only to rise and begin the routine again.

Just weeks after her initiation into prostitution, Khady and her friend were arrested for practicing illegally. Not wanting their names on file, they had not registered with the police. They were put in prison and forced to register. For four days Khady slept in a barren cell, dreading what her father would do when he found out. Her sister eventually found and freed her after going to the fish processing factory and learning Khady had never worked there. As they walked home, Khady begged her sister to keep her secret from their father. "We told my mother because mothers can hold things in for you that fathers cannot," Khady remembered.

After her time in prison Khady was convinced that her mother's three co-wives had put a spell on her so that she would become a prostitute. Co-wives often bring about evil, she said, by going to a *marabout* and telling him they want something bad to happen to you. "Once this happens, there is nothing you can do. You can go to another *marabout* to reverse it, but that did not work for me," Khady insisted sadly. "The other wives turned my heart against my family, so I had to leave." Had she stayed and her father and his co-wives discovered Khady's secret, he might have divorced her mother. "What you do or do not do is blamed on your mother. I did not want to cause her problems, so I told the family I was going to buy cloth in Mauritania to sell in Dakar."

Khady divorced her second husband and left town with her prostitute friend. Once in Mauritania she actually did buy and sell cloth, but the profit was not enough to keep her in food, lodging, and sufficient capital to purchase more cloth. Supplementing the commerce of cloth with commerce of her body, she supported herself until she married her third husband, a Senegalese businessman, and had a daughter. Relying on him for financial support, she stopped seeking clients and concentrated on her own small business and caring for their new baby. Years later they were forced to leave Mauritania and had no place to go other than her parents' home.

When her father argued that her third husband could never adequately support her and their daughter because he lost his business, Khady retorted, "if he's going to eat sand, I'm going to eat it with him. It's not nice to leave someone." She and her new family left Dakar and moved south to the holy city of Touba. Three months later Khady did leave her husband, not to fulfill her father's wishes, but because her husband had begun to drink heavily and often abused her. She took her daughter to her family in Dakar then headed to Kaolack to look for prostitute friends who were working there.

RHAMA

One of the women Khady found was Rhama, a friendly yet serious woman who conducted her life with an air of purpose and determination. Even larger than Khady and much prettier, Rhama entered prostitution after escaping three destructive marriages. Shortly before the expulsion of Senegalese from Mauritania, Rhama left Mauritania to visit her mother. Because of the border disputes, she was not able to return to her house there. She lost everything, including an expensive car she had bought with years of savings.

Unlike Khady, Rhama never knew her father, who died shortly before her birth in 1953. Alone, her mother raised her and her siblings. Decades later, Rhama remained angry at her mother for not sending her to school. "Didn't she know I'd be able to do nothing but prostitute?" she asked rhetorically. Despite her lack of education, Rhama spoke excellent French and was the designated accountant for a fund set aside by twelve of the Ndangane women. Each week the women contributed 2000 CFA (approximately ten dollars). At the end of the month, one woman received the entire amount to spend as she wished. In an emergency, the women went to Rhama and made a case for a loan, to be paid back as soon as possible.

Rhama also helped Ndangane women not rich or responsible enough to form such a group by loaning them money. They were known by Rhama and Khady as "the drinkers" and were pitied, if not respected. Khady, who was also very generous to them, criticized them for drinking—a sin according to Islam. "I'm already a prostitute and I smoke. That's bad enough. Why drink also?"

TAKING CHARGE OF SEXUAL RELATIONS

As prostitutes, Rhama and Khady had much to lose and nothing to gain by recounting their life stories and revealing details about their families. My strategy of staying at the clinic for several months before spending much time in Ndangane seemed to have paid off. Their eventual trust of me and my intentions led them to accept my request for their services as language and cultural translators. They generously took time to tell me their stories and to translate those of other women when I began life history interviews. I learned much through observing their interactions with colleagues and was deeply impressed by their integrity and compassion. Khady was occasionally concerned that I would be angry when she interrupted our discussions to accommodate a client. I continually told her that it was I who did not want to interrupt her work. When a client arrived I moved to a chair outside her hut or visited an unoccupied prostitute. Although I knew work meant money, I was ambivalent as I watched the flow of clientele through Khady's door. On the one hand, the more clients she had, the sooner she could afford to leave the profession. On the other hand, it bothered me to think about what she endured behind those thatch walls.

I did not have to imagine for very long, as Khady and other women were quick to tell me what they permitted and did not permit clients to do during sex. Khady said women often tricked men into thinking they were having intercourse when the men had not actually entered the women, who used their thighs to simulate intercourse. "It's really easy for fat women because men can't really see what's going on down there," she said. The women always left on their multiple layers—a *boubou* and one or more *pagne* wrapped around like skirts—when they were with clients. These several yards of cloth obstructed men's view of the women's bodies. Using this to their advantage, the women avoided potential HIV infection by preventing fluids from entering their bodies when they did not feel like arguing with a client about condom use or were sore from frequent intercourse.

Interestingly, the women's sexual preferences prior to the advent of AIDS facilitated the adoption of safe sex practices. For instance, the women claimed to have refused oral and anal sex, which are potentially more dangerous because men are more reluctant to wear condoms during these activities than during vaginal intercourse. Since these activities are highly stigmatized in Senegal, it is difficult to determine if the prostitutes were being completely honest in their denial. Still, anecdotal evidence supported their statements that they limited their contacts with clients to vaginal intercourse long before the advent of AIDS. This preference was due more to cultural attitudes and lack of enjoyment than to the potential for disease transmission. In fact, the women were fearful that clients might "eat" them when performing oral sex. This suspicion stemmed from beliefs that *deme* (devils) were most likely to prey on victims when they were nude. *Deme* were thought to "eat" people from the inside out, weakening and eventually killing them. Making a sour face, Khady commented that she might agree to oral and anal sex with her fiance, but never with a stranger, who might be a *deme*.

Khady's fiancé weighed half as much as she. Equally small in character, he continued to make unfulfilled promises to find a job so he could afford to marry her. For three years she had paid the rent for their room, which was in a house owned by a resident of Ndangane. Three other prostitutes lived in adjoining rooms, two with their boyfriends. They used the terms "fiancé" and "boyfriend" interchangeably to signify supposed monogamy and intent to marry. Rhama and Fatou warned me against having such relationships. "The men just take advantage of you and take your money," Fatou explained. "If he says he loves you, make him marry you. None of this fiancé business." She waved a hand toward Maty who remained "engaged" to an unemployed man for twenty years.

When I casually mentioned that I had left a boyfriend after a stormy relationship, the group of women sharing lunch with me smiled not at the information, but because I had confided in them. It was then that I realized that they had many questions to ask me, but had not out of courtesy, even though I often asked them invasive questions.

That I had lived with a man whom I left changed their view of me. Younger than they and relatively reserved, they assumed I was "innocent." I told them about my past relationships, though I could only smile from embarrassment when they made graphic gestures with their hands, mouths, and other parts of their bodies to determine the extent to which I had been involved with a man. When I added that I was dating Michael, Fatou repeated her advice about marriage, now more sure than ever that men all over the world can be dangerous.

FATOU

Fatou told me she learned all about men during her four marriages, three of which were polygamous. She was pregnant nine times and had six living children, all of whom she supported without assistance from former husbands. At the end of each month she sent money to her mother, who cared for the children in Dakar. Fatou's skepticism about men manifested itself in every aspect of her life. She warned other women that clients' condoms could not be trusted because she had witnessed first-hand that they reused or purposely put holes in condoms so they would burst during intercourse. This was clients' way of forcing women to continue sexual relations without protection, she said. I guessed that the wooden club in the corner of her hut might help deter a client up to these tricks. She grinned mischievously then sighed, "Men."

A few days earlier Fatou's older sister, Saye, had trouble convincing a client to wear a condom. With the reinforcement of Fatou and other colleagues, Saye talked him into complying. After he left, Saye emerged from her hut holding a used condom. She showed the contents to Fatou and the other women who had gathered. The condom contained very dark fluid. "You are very lucky he wore a condom," Fatou remarked. "Show this to the drinkers so they'll remember to use condoms."

SAYE

Saye, a small, gentle woman with a dark, inch-wide tattoo around the outside of her mouth—revealing that she underwent a painful Fulbe rite of passage as a teenager in the 1940's—worked in the hut some twenty feet across the dirt compound from her sister. She referred to me as her daughter and was very happy to meet my mother, who visited a few months after I began spending time in Ndangane. Following the visit, Saye always asked how my mother was, as is the custom. But, having met my mother added new meaning to the question for Saye and me.

Forming such relationships was important to Saye and the other women in Ndangane, most of whom had left their children with relatives and lived alone or with mere acquaintances in Kaolack. In a society where family and community are so strongly emphasized, Ndangane prostitutes developed familial relationships and used kinship terms for their new friends, whom they called sisters, daughters, and mothers. During my time in Ndangane, I gained three mothers, seven sisters, countless cousins, a Godchild named after me, and a few marriage proposals from some of the women's clients and vendors passing through the neighborhood.

Although Fatou and Saye had the same father and different mothers, the details were irrelevant; they were simply sisters. They led similar lives, they said, because their father, a prominent *marabout*, forbade them to go to school. They blamed him for their inability to find more respectable work, pointing to their successful, educated sisters. These other "sisters" were relatives whose fathers permitted them to attend school. "*Marabouts*," explained Fatou and Saye, "are good men, but they make lousy fathers" due to their allegiance to tradition. In the past it might have been acceptable to keep girls out of school so they could learn to be good housewives, commented the forty-something sisters, but with the rampant rise of divorce, urban migration, and the cost of living, women need to learn useful skills to earn needed income. It is ironic that the most religious of men, adhering to the strictest of rules, may have inadvertently played a role in their daughters' commission of one of Islam's most serious transgressions, adultery.

TAKING ONE DAY AT A TIME: DAILY STRUGGLES

After talking to the sisters, I drove to my house a few miles away. As I pulled into the driveway, Malick, a five-year-old the size of someone half his age, ran down the dirt road to greet me. Keeping with our daily ritual, he hopped onto my lap and together we drove around the block, listening to American music on my tape deck as he waved to our neighbors. When we pulled back into my driveway he jumped out with the excitement of a child getting off the roller coaster at Disneyland. He ran to the end of the garage and, with elaborate gestures, directed me into my parking spot. Before I finished greeting Mbodj, Malick disappeared down the dirt road.

Although my mother almost cried when she saw my house and neighborhood, I was living in the relative lap of luxury. Running water, electricity, a telephone, and a bathtub made my three-bedroom stucco house a haven for my neighbors and Peace Corps volunteers passing through town. Reflecting on the women's stories as I took a bath to wash off the Ndangane dirt, I compared the women's lives with my own. Our outer worlds were vastly different but our inner worlds were much the same. I could easily relate to their basic dilemmas associated with earning money, developing relationships, and warding off the stress of everyday life, but the difference in the degree to which these concerns controlled our separate lives was enormous.

PURSUIT OF CONDOMS

Fear of HIV infection did not keep me up nights as it did the prostitutes. Days after being tested for HIV in the United States, I knew my status. These women had been tested years earlier and still did not know the results. For condoms, all I needed to do was walk into the embassy's health clinic and take a handful from a basket on the desk. No limit, no payment, no questions asked. A Senegalese woman had to buy condoms directly from a nurse at the STD and family planning clinics or from pharmacists kept them hidden behind a counter in the busy pharmacy. Whereas the prostitutes felt comfortable getting condoms from clinic staff, both prostitutes and non-prostitutes were concerned that a pharmacist would criticize them for asking for the stigmatized product. Whether or not pharmacists were passing judgment, women were very reluctant to approach them because of the shame and guilt they felt. Rather than walk a block to the pharmacy, the Ndangane women paid a dollar for a taxi ride to the clinic, bought condoms at prices subject to the whim of clinic staff, and paid a dollar to return home. The trip cost roughly the same amount as they earned from two clients.

POWER-PLAYS WITH CLINIC STAFF

Attempts to convince clinic staff to provide additional free condoms per visit were fruitless. The most common excuse they offered was that they did not want the women to sell the condoms. Based on the women's reported number of partners, the staff's concerns were unsubstantiated. The staff also were concerned that supplies of condoms would run out, although sources in Dakar indicated that there were warehouses full of aging condoms that needed to be used before their expiration date. The prostitutes' frustration grew each time they went into the examining room, where a case of one thousand condoms was stored under the table.

Disagreement about condom distribution added to the tension between the women and clinic staff, creating further distance between the health-care providers and the at-risk health-care recipients. The prostitutes resented clinic staff for withholding such an important commodity, while clinic staff likened the resentful prostitutes to rebellious children in need of parental control. The prostitutes often felt powerless dealing with the staff, who in many ways dictated their physical and mental health.

The laboratory technician was especially disliked for his alleged blackmailing of the prostitutes. According to them, he threatened to lie about their health if they did not give him a bribe before he examined their urine and vaginal smear samples. The women felt trapped, knowing that an STD diagnosis would cost them their registration cards until they received a negative test report. No card meant no business and no income. He also took money from them by selling them condoms, which were supposed to be free. Often, he left several boxes of condoms with Rhama and Khady, who sold them then gave him their earnings. The women reasoned it was better to submit to him than to risk having no condoms at all.

The technician's mother and sister benefitted financially through dealings with the prostitutes as well. Years ago, his mother bought several of the work huts from their original owners and charged rent for their use. She also owned a small restaurant adjacent to the huts. Her daughter cooked meals, which they sold to the prostitutes and their clients. When clinic staff raised the issue of helping the prostitutes find other means of income and alternative housing, the technician maintained the women did not need such help. His transparent arguments revealed his fear of financial loss should the prostitutes no longer need his family.

In December, Senegal hosted the International AIDS in Africa Conference in Dakar. When I returned to Kaolack after attending the conference the women anxiously told me that they had been without condoms for more than a week. According to them, the entire clinic staff had closed the clinic and gone to the conference, leaving no condoms behind. When the staff returned they said they had handed out what remained of their supply before leaving Kaolack. Still, they returned from Dakar empty-handed, fully aware that no one but they could or would deliver needed condoms from the Dakar warehouse.

Although I did not want to take sides, the staff's actions and attitudes indicated little concern for the women's welfare. It is true that transporting the condoms would have been complicated and costly because they did not have their own vehicles and a case of condoms would not fit in a taxi's trunk. As a result, the staff would have to pay a taxi driver extra to tie the box to the roof or they would have to track down a driver with a sta-

tion wagon, which was even more expensive. In all, they would
have had to take a taxi to the warehouse, pay extra for another
taxi to take them and the box to the Dakar transport station, pay
extra for the bus or taxi ride to Kaolack, then pay extra for a taxi
ride from the Kaolack transport station to the clinic. But supply-
ing condoms had become part of their job since the woman who
had originally done it quit and was not replaced. Why she was
not replaced was a question never answered. Even so, was not
the women's welfare more important than the occasional has-
sle? Easy for me to ask. Still, how could the women be expected
to heed the staff's safe sex advice if they had no condoms? It
was especially frustrating for me to hear of this situation only
days after attending a conference session in which the staff reported their AIDS prevention campaign's success.

The following weekend Michael visited Kaolack and
brought a case of one thousand condoms. We delivered it to
the clinic then drove straight to Ndangane to inform the
women of its arrival. I secretly wished we had taken the case
directly to the women, but it was important for me to go
through proper channels. The head nurse was already annoyed by my trips to the Chief of Police and the Regional
Medical Officer with Ibra, whom she did not like. Yet each day
it became more and more difficult for me to remain impartial.

Weighing the ethical implications of trying to change the
prostitutes' situation, I decided that I should continue showing the women I supported them by conveying their concerns
to clinic staff and Dr. Mboup. I also decided that it was my
responsibility to convey clinic staff's concerns to Dr. Mboup
and others in Dakar, and resigned to continue doing so in as
diplomatic a manner as I could. Beyond that, I felt that being
blatantly critical of the clinic staff and the politics affecting dis-
semination of condoms could backfire, possibly causing people to be angry with me and with each other. This could
jeopardize already fragile relationships and worsen the situation. Knowing I would be leaving in a few months and did

not have a mechanism for remaining directly involved in the women's lives, alerting people to the needs and problems I identified and providing recommendations for meeting them was the most constructive contribution I could make. Whether clinic staff and decision makers in Dakar would take my advice was their choice. I could still help and support the women, I told myself, but it would be unfair to promise drastic change in such a complicated system.

Still, I helped the prostitutes when I could. When Couna pleaded with me for condoms, I handed her a handful from a box under the head nurse's desk. She tucked them into the front of her *pagne*. I looked around to be sure no one was around, then handed her more and more condoms until her *pagne* was bulging as if she were pregnant. We laughed at the sight.

"And I'm in menopause," she whispered as she patted her stomach.

"Share them with your friends," I whispered back.

"Consider it done, Sow. Thank you," she winked as she left.

"Noko bokk," I responded. We're all in it together.

COUNA AND FATIMATA

Couna, a substitute mother to younger women like Rhama and Khady, moved to Ndangane with her sister Maty in the 1950's. She changed her name to Couna so that visiting friends and relatives, who believed she worked in a restaurant, would not be able to find her among the prostitutes. Ironically, her given name was identical to that of one of her prostitute neighbors.

Unlike many other women, Couna never left Ndangane nor did she stop practicing prostitution once she started. "She's a chronic prostitute," Khady commented. Maty remained with Couna for decades after Maty stopped practicing prostitution due to illness. She and Couna struck a deal: Couna would earn the income and Maty would do the cooking and cleaning in the house they shared with Couna's unemployed fiance.

Couna did very well as a prostitute when she was younger, earning her the distinction of being the only woman whose hut had two rooms. At her suggestion, I occasionally used the first as a waiting room while she finished with a client in the second. Dozens of *gris-gris*—charms made of herbs, bones and pieces of paper scrawled with passages from the Koran—hung above the doorway to attract high-paying customers and keep away trouble. A strong believer in the power of traditional practices, Couna sprinkled a mixture of herbs and water on the dirt in front of her hut each morning. She then splashed the remainder on her bare neck and chest, muttering a prayer for a good day, a way out of prostitution, and money to replace her son's broken-down taxi.

Fatimata, who worked in the hut next door, greeted Couna each morning as she arrived for work.

"I hope that there is nothing bad," she would say as they shook hands.

"No," Couna would reply. "There is peace only."

"Thanks be to God," Fatimata would say sincerely.

"Thanks be to God," Couna would repeat, overlapping Fatimata's words.

The two women had known each other for as many years as Couna worked in Ndangane. They were both in their late fifties and attracted the same clientele. Through time, they developed a friendly rivalry in their attempts to attract customers. At the beginning, Fatimata consistently had more clients than Couna. This was due in part to the fact that Fatimata, a Mandinka, was circumcised at puberty. Men who believed an uncircumcised woman was impure and unfeminine preferred her over Couna and other uncircumcised women.

When Fatimata, a soft spoken woman with big, beautiful brown eyes and a fragile build, began earning more money than her neighbor, she would dance in front of the huts, singing of her success. On those occasions when Couna received more clients, a smile would light up her tired eyes and round, puffy face as she would dance, sing, and laugh all the more.

The clinic doctor surmised that Maty and Fatimata shared many of the same clients because they often were infected with the same STDs at the same time. Both were HIV positive and, as evidenced by their recurring infections, they did not always require their partners to wear condoms despite their insistence that they did.

"That Couna," Khady said angrily when the topic of condom use came up. "She'll take any man and she'll take anything in exchange for sex. We set the minimum at three hundred francs (about one dollar), but she'll take a hundred and fifty. She'll take batteries, matches, clothes. She's asking for AIDS."

At least two years after clinic staff knew that Fatimata, Couna, and some one hundred and twenty other Kaolack prostitutes were HIV positive, the women still had not been informed of their status. Citing inability to deal with the women's reactions to an HIV-positive test result, the employees were waiting until they felt that the women were knowledgeable enough about AIDS and its implications to handle the news. The staff clearly dreaded telling the women their status. Asked the doctor, "How do you tell someone she is going to die?".

At the doctor's request, I developed two questionnaires to help prepare staff for telling the women their HIV status. The first was designed to assess how the women might react to an HIV-positive diagnosis, to whom they would talk about it, and whether they would remain in Kaolack for counseling and treatment. The second questionnaire was administered by staff a month after the women learned their status to determine how the women were handling the news.

Interestingly, whereas staff withheld registration cards of STD-infected prostitutes, they did not confiscate registration cards of HIV-infected women. They reasoned that this would probably lead the women to leave town to practice prostitution covertly. In leaving, the women would no longer attend the clinic for health examinations and would not have access to free condoms. Therefore, rather than turn the women away, staff encouraged seropositive women to continue working and living as they had and stressed all the more the importance of condom use. They told infected women that they not only had to protect their partners, but that they would become more ill if exposed to the virus again. Staff also urged the women to go to them for medical treatment when possible, and to tell other doctors of their status if they went to them for treatment. They told the story of an HIV-positive prostitute who went to the hospital and failed to tell the doctor she was infected. According to staff, the doctor gave her medicine that inadvertently killed her.

Not surprisingly, every woman walked out of her private meeting with clinic staff (all members of the staff knew each woman's status) and told her colleagues that her test results were negative. A few HIV-positive women did confide in their families and boyfriends, but most preferred to talk to clinic staff when they needed to vent their fear and anger. When Sadio, my first interviewee, learned she was HIV positive, she began showing up at the head nurse's house at all hours of the day hoping to talk about her anxiety. The head nurse listened to her, but said Sadio could not keep this up. So, Sadio visited Maria until Maria said she could not accept visitors after hours, then visited the assistant nurse until she was told the same. She was fast running out of people to confide in, and the anxiety would not subside. Although I would have liked to talk with the women about their experiences, it was not my place, and I only knew of their status when clinic staff accidentally said something revealing.

Fatimata reacted differently to the news she was HIV positive. When she began to weaken, she told her family she had syphilis. Knowing she could not hide the fact that she was sick, she wanted to spare them the shame and stigma of being related to a person with AIDS. She died only one month after hearing her diagnosis. Couna mourned the loss of her friend and rival, giving strict orders that Fatimata's work hut should remain empty.

Fatimata's was not the first AIDS death Couna witnessed, although it was never officially confirmed that any of the prostitutes' deaths were due to AIDS. When Couna's sister, Maty, became very ill, she asked Couna to take her home to their village. Many of the women said they would do the same thing if they fell ill, preferring to die in their birthplace rather than in an unfriendly hospital or in dirty Ndangane. Couna's daughter and mother took care of Maty, not knowing she was HIV positive. Couna suspected, and kept a safe distance from her sister when she visited. "I don't want to get infected," Couna explained. "I have children to support."

Couna was not alone in her fear of being near people living with AIDS. Although the clinic staff repeatedly explained to the women that the virus is not spread through casual contact, they also made a point of saying that one could never be too careful, advising them to avoid sharing clothes, *cure dents*, and eating utensils. When I questioned the doctor's strategy he said that it was better to scare the women about AIDS than to allow them to ignore their risk. What resulted, however, was paranoia preventing them from caring for sick colleagues and friends who desperately needed them. HIV-positive women would not even consent to meeting for group counseling, fearful that the word would get out and their friends would ostracize them. "When you are seropositive you should put it in your heart and leave it there," Khady said.

When Couna learned her daughter had used Maty's *cure dent* she worried constantly that her daughter might be infected, blaming herself for not warning her. According to Couna, Maty might have cut her gums, which could have bled onto the *cure dent*, which could have then infected Maty's daughter if she rubbed the blood into her own gums. The likelihood of this happening is so minute that most doctors dismiss its possibility.

MATY

As Khady and I walked to the work huts after offering our condolences to Couna the day after Maty's death, Khady told me Maty's story. Maty had been very mean to her boyfriends, Khady recalled. The first had no family and was suffering from cancer. "Maty would not give him money or buy him a blanket. He was cold all the time, so thin and weak. When he died she kept all his things and gave his family nothing." The second boyfriend died of AIDS. "She took him home to his village and left him there. Wouldn't even visit. Can you imagine, Coumba? Not visiting your boyfriend? She was bad."

"Do you think she got AIDS from the boyfriend?" I asked.

"Maybe. Anyway, bad people get AIDS. She was bad so God punished her. Good people do not suffer long and painful deaths."

"But what if a good person gets AIDS?".

"Then you wonder why God would punish her. AIDS is the worst punishment of all."

"So has God already planned your death?" I asked.

"Yes, I think so."

"Well, if it's not supposed to be from AIDS, why are you so careful about not getting infected?"

"I avoid it with all my power, then the rest is up to God. I also try to be a good person. There is more to life than the time we spend on earth. When I die I will ask God's forgiveness for my sin of prostitution, and he will know I have always been good."

Khady and the other women tried so hard to be "good," to play the roles expected of them as Senegalese women and mothers while living very different lives from their own mothers and other female relatives they admired as girls. They realized their circumstances were different and required different actions, which demanded that they take charge of their lives and destinies in ways that most Senegalese women were spared. Although they had been raised to depend on men for all or partial support, they found themselves with only themselves to depend on and consequently turned to prostitution, believing it to be their only option. Participation in the stigmatized profession required them to become more independent due to physical and philosophical separation from their families, whom they wanted to protect from the shame of their work.

A few of the women, such as Khady, Rhama and Sadio, felt the need not only to take charge of their own lives but of their prostitute community's survival as well. Like the men who protected the villages in which they were raised, these women took upon the roles of leaders and protectors, pushing for fair treatment and an environment in which they could safely live and work. Ironically, their growing solidarity and devotion to the community conflicted with their inherent disrespect for the factor that drew the women together in the first place: prostitution. The next chapter examines the ways in which the women sought to reconcile their beliefs that God might punish them for their work with their conviction that they were taking charge of their lives to the best of their abilities.

4

Praying for Forgiveness

You can pray from Ndangane, but God won't answer you.
— Maria (clinic nurse)

ON BEING A REAL MUSLIM

Khady talked of prayer the way I talked of wishes and day-dreams. Praying, she implied, made a dream more likely to come true. She believed in God's power over life, death, and eternal fate. She also believed that asking his forgiveness for the sin of prostitution would enable her to go to paradise, so she asked him for it in Wolof each morning and evening. This type of praying was different from the way she prayed when she was growing up in her father's house. There, she covered her head, cleansed her body, put a prayer mat on the ground, and faced Mecca. She then went through the sequence of standing, kneeling, and supplicating while uttering verses from the Koran in Arabic. As an adult, the only time she practiced this ritual was when she went home to see her parents. "At my father's house you don't eat if you don't pray," she said simply.

Although all the prostitutes I interviewed identified themselves as Muslim, most of the women in Ndangane abandoned the outward manifestations of their religion. They did not pray five times a day, as required. They did not plan to travel to Mecca, even if they eventually saved enough money to do so. They rarely gave alms to the poor. But they continued to revere one God, Allah, and to accept Mohammed as his prophet. These activities (the pillars of Islam) are seen by most Muslims as pivotal to observing the faith. Although prostitution did not directly prevent the women from performing the first three activities, it did pose physical and emotional barriers. Some women allowed these barriers to limit their religious practice while others did all they could to overcome them.

NENE

Nene worked in the bars and hotels in town. She never wanted to work in Ndangane because it was a place of sin. Besides, she explained, she could make much more money from the clients she met in fancier locations. She dressed accordingly, in elaborate, richly colored *boubous* of royal blue and burgundy, and thick gold necklaces, bracelets, and earrings. Her make-up was always perfectly applied to her bronze skin and her lips seemed permanently dark red. Neither she nor the women who worked in Ndangane fit the common stereotype of a prostitute. The difference, however, was that, rather than looking like village matrons as the Ndangane women did, Nene and many of her in-town colleagues could be mistaken for upper-middle-class wives of government employees. And in many respects, Nene lived the family life of one. Central to her lifestyle was religion. Nene prayed five times a day with her family, with whom she lived. She celebrated holidays with them, cooking meals, dancing to drums, and going to mosque.

On ordinary days, she performed ordinary chores. She would wash laundry by hand, pound millet in a large mortar, iron clothes with a coal-burning iron, and bargain at the market for each day's food. At night, however, she would sleep only a few hours before sneaking out of the compound to take a taxi to the sector of town that was just waking up. She would accept two or three clients an hour for several hours then tiptoe home to sleep. In the morning she would rise with her family and dole out her earnings a little bit at a time, claiming she made the money selling cloth, perfume, and jewelry.

By the time she was forty years old, Nene saved enough money to make the pilgrimage to Mecca. This was a rarity for a woman her age. When she went to the Saudi Arabian Embassy to get a visa, they asked her if she had ever been arrested. Yes, she said, when she was a clandestine prostitute many years ago. She was taken to prison in Dakar because she was not registered. The embassy's consul told her that she could not receive a visa until she withdrew her registration from the police and the STD clinic in Dakar. The next day, she delivered a letter requesting withdrawal to the clinic. She then underwent a battery of STD tests and waited for her results. When the clinic approved her withdrawal, she took documentation to the police department, who stamped her file to indicate she was no longer registered and should be imprisoned if found practicing. This done, Nene returned to the embassy and was granted a visa. She flew to Saudi Arabia the same day.

Nene traveled to Mecca to walk on the ground where the prophet once walked and to pray in the mosque where millions of Muslims pay homage to him. It was the most wonderful experience of her life. When she returned to Senegal, she did not need to re-register in Dakar; she had been registered in Kaolack for years under a different name.

Nene's story left me with many questions about the connection between the women's actions on earth and their consequences in life after death. Khady said that prostitutes are rarely taken to the mosque when they die. Simply put, those not taken to the mosque will not be pardoned by God for their sins and will not go to paradise. Interestingly, it is neither God nor the individual who ultimately decides where the deceased will go; it is the person's community. Normally, the community accepts that every woman who has practiced Islam during her life will be taken to the mosque. But when her integrity and faith are in question, there may be serious discussion about her final destination. Usually the *marabout* who presides over the funeral makes the decision, but he asks the woman's family members and neighbors about her conduct during her time on earth.

According to the prostitutes and clinic staff, a woman's community may question why she never married or remained single long after being divorced or widowed. If she remained single so that she could care for her parents, siblings, or other relatives' children, she is praised and taken to the mosque. If, on the other hand, the *marabout* hears from community members that the woman provoked divorce, was involved with many men, or did not practice Islam regularly, she probably will not receive his blessing.

The prostitutes feared this fate. That is why they hid their work from their family and friends, often moved hundreds of miles from their children to live among strangers, and prayed daily for a way out. Ironically, many felt that they were prostitutes because that is what God wanted them to do. Others acknowledged openly that they were committing a sin: "There is a contradiction between Islam and the work that I do," said one. Another offered: "Islam does not like this profession at all. No one should accept it."

Thus, the women struggled with accepting themselves and pardoning their own actions while criticizing prostitution from a Muslim perspective. Many caught in this hypocrisy still called themselves "real Muslims." I asked the social worker about the prostitutes' definition of themselves.

"There are two kinds of Muslims: those who pray and those who don't," he said.

"Are both kinds 'real Muslims'?"

"No. Those who do not pray are not real Muslims and will not go to heaven."

"What if they pray, but practice prostitution?"

"Real worshipers are not going to prostitute themselves after praying."

By extension, many prostitutes and non-prostitutes believed that real worshipers were less inclined to contract HIV and that prostitutes were more prone to HIV infection than are other people. The clinic doctor explained the prevailing attitude: "Not only are people going to hell for sinning, but God is beginning to punish them on earth with AIDS." Another clinic employee said, "AIDS is seen as a divine punishment against those who no longer serve God as they should." Another employee observed, "God does nothing bad."

NDIEME

"I am a real Muslim," Ndieme, an older, in-town prostitute, declared during our first interview. She pulled her soft, dark brown hair from her face with one hand and held a *cure dent* with the other, rubbing her teeth between sentences. "I take care of my children. I have a beautiful house. I buy a large sack of rice at the end of every month." I asked about her house, described by clinic staff as spacious and nicely decorated—a stark contrast to the barren single rooms inhabited by Ndangane prostitutes. "Prostitution helped me buy the house, and commerce helped me furnish it," she explained proudly. "I do personal commerce." Such commerce included prostitution and selling beauty products. She prided herself most on the fact that she chose her clients, rather than the other way around. "I am not like those women in Ndangane who grab any man who walks by. I decide who will come to my house." Rather than go to hotel rooms, she preferred to take her clients to her house when her children were gone or asleep. She was extremely secretive about her work, shielding her children from it in every way possible. During our first interview she repeated that the name she registered under was her daughter's name, which should not be used in print. She also kept warning me not to take a picture of her, lest it appear in a book that her scholarly daughter might read. I did not have a camera with me and had never mentioned photography to her.

Steadying myself for a strong reaction, I asked how she reconciled prostitution with her devotion to Islam. "I am a good Muslim and a good mother. Prostitution is the only way I could care for my children when I left my husband. I hated his other three wives. So better to be a prostitute than to let my babies starve. God will forgive me. I buy a big sack of rice every month, you know." Rice is a luxury, and her pride in affording it conveyed the importance of caring for her children and succeeding on her own.

Ndieme was very strict about condom use. "When you're sick from AIDS everyone rejects you, even your mother. So I avoid it with all my power." When asked how she dealt with reluctant clients, she acted out a hypothetical scene. "If he crosses his arms and says 'No,' I look him in the eyes and I say 'You, you don't love your life. If you did you wouldn't act so stupid!' Then, if he still resists, I show him the door," she pointed dramatically to the door. "Goodbye!" she waved to the imaginary stupid man.

AMY

Amy, also a prostitute in town, regarded herself as very religious, yet she viewed her responsibility to her community and family much differently than did Ndieme. She did not have children, but relied on prostitution to support her and her mother, with whom she lived. Amy's father died when she was young, requiring Amy's mother to work as a maid until she was too old and weak to continue. After telling her mother that she decided to become a prostitute, Amy registered at the STD clinic near their Kaolack home. "Yes, my mother knows. I keep no secrets from her," Amy told me as we sat on wobbly metal chairs in a sparse examining room at the clinic. Because Amy was loud and adamant, Khady looked into the room to see what was going on. Unlike most women I interviewed, Amy did not stop mid-sentence when others were within hearing distance. She looked at Khady as she continued. "I think prostitutes should say what they are doing. No more lies."

Amy believed that as a good Muslim she should not add to the problems of the world. "Prostitutes should not have children," she stated. On one of her visits to the clinic for an examination, the head nurse noticed that Amy, a few months pregnant, had an infection. When the STD tests came back negative the head nurse told Amy that whatever the infection was, it looked serious. She urged Amy to take some antibiotics, but Amy declined and left the clinic. A few hours later, she returned with her mother and announced that the baby had "spontaneously" aborted. When pressed further, Amy admitted that she and her mother had done something to bring it about. This was at least her second abortion.

As philosophical and adamant about sex as she was about religion and prostitution, Amy set limits regarding the type of sex in which she would engage with clients. No anal or oral intercourse. "Those activities are not normal, especially anal intercourse. That is what homosexuals do. If a woman is going to give oral sex, the man must still wear a condom. But I won't do that, even when the men offer extra money. I just have normal intercourse for money, share it with my mom, and live my life as a good Muslim."

AISSATOU

Aissatou, a feeble woman whose high cheekbones and long, sinewy neck hinted at her fading beauty, approached Khady and me as we ate peanuts and watched the sun set into the dust beyond the edge of town. "Sit down!" Khady said to Aissatou in English. Khady used the phrase whenever she could; it was the only one she remembered from school. Not understanding, Aissatou sat down anyway, obviously exhausted by the walk from the clinic to Ndangane in the heat. She did not so much as glance at our peanuts, as this was the second day of Ramadan, the Muslim holiday during which followers are supposed to abstain from food and other pleasures from sunrise to sunset for a month. "Soon you will be able to eat," Khady comforted her as she shelled another peanut and popped in her mouth. "The sun is on its way down."

Aissatou looked at the sun, lost in thought. She seemed too fragile to subject herself to the burden of fasting and, judging from the excuses others offered for not observing the holiday, she surely would have been forgiven for preserving her health. "Ramadan is so difficult," she remarked more to the sun than to us.

"You should eat," I said. "You don't look well."

"Oh, I'm fine. I mean Ramadan is hard because there is no money."

Observing Ramadan meant the women might go hungry, not so much due to lack of food, but because sex—which is pleasure of the flesh—was forbidden during the day. For a Ndangane prostitute, this was a fifty percent cut in income. Prostitutes who did not fast and did not abstain from intercourse with clients also suffered financially during this period because clients tended to stay closer to home day and night. Their burden, however, was not as heavy as that of women who adamantly refused to break religious rules. When I asked Aissatou why she and one other woman were the only

Ndangane prostitutes to observe Ramadan, she replied that perhaps the other women could not afford to forego the money they made from clients during the day.

Aissatou's religious adherence was profound. She went to Ndangane only to work and carried herself like a saint. She maintained a physical and emotional distance from the other prostitutes and never entered their frequent disputes. When she sat next to me and Khady it was truly a rare incident, signaling that she could not make it to her hut without resting. Normally, she would have waved at us in acknowledgment without stopping to shake hands or strike up conversation.

When I first interviewed her about her life, Aissatou looked straight at me, tears in her eyes, and pleaded for a way out of prostitution. "I am an old lady. People will not even say hello to me on the street," she cried. "But I would do anything if it meant leaving prostitution. I can't even stand to hear that word," she cringed. Prostitution. She had grown up in a Muslim household and had obeyed her *marabout's* every word. She married a prominent military officer, raised law-abiding children, and prayed five times a day without exception. She cleansed herself ritually. She stayed away from the mosque when she was menstruating. She never ate pork, smoked, nor drank. She even resisted braiding fake hair (*mesh*) into her own to make it more attractive and full. "The *marabouts* say it is not right to change what God has given you. God gave me thin hair, and he does not want me to add something artificial to it." Likewise, she never tried *xessal*, a cream that bleaches the skin to make it lighter and more attractive to men. "I don't want to be white. God made me black. He also made me thin, and you thin, and her fat," she pointed to Khady who smiled smugly, proud of her two hundred plus pounds. "Men say they prefer fat women with large bottoms. Not for me. I am not going to eat peanuts or avoid fasting to be big."

A feminist and a compliant Muslim woman—it seems contradictory, I thought. She was not one to mince words, but she was one to follow to the letter those that were written in the Koran and spoken by her *marabout*. "So what is a nice woman like you doing in a place like this? " I wanted to ask to lighten the mood. Instead, she started to explain on her own. That half hour before the sun disappears is the hardest on the mind and stomach, so better to preoccupy them with a good story.

Aissatou was married for years to a monogamous man who treated her very well. "He never beat me, he didn't smoke. He didn't go to prostitutes or anything. Truly the most honorable of men," she told the sun. "Then he died suddenly, left behind my only child and me," she shook her head from side to side, signalling the tragedy of it all. "We got a little bit of insurance money, but not enough. I tried to start a business, but it was too expensive and I made too little. I prayed and prayed for an answer. The only answer was prostitution.

"'God,' I said one day. 'God, I have been a good woman all my life. I have obeyed you and your words. I have resisted temptation. What do I do now?' No answer. But the next day I ran into another widow who had started prostitution. And that seemed to be my answer." Aissatou reasoned that she would change her life to support herself and her son, but that all else would remain the same. She viewed prostitution as a temporary situation to hold her over until her son could support her. Twenty years later, Aissatou was still practicing because her son's income as a factory worker was barely enough to support his wife and several children.

"Aissatou prays from Ndangane?," Maria asked incredulously when I visited the clinic the following day. "Well, " she reflected, "I guess you can pray from Ndangane but God is not going to answer you. It's a place of sin. What interest in it and them would God have? It's so dirty there that you cannot even purify yourself. It's better to wait until you get home at night and pray there."

"But you're supposed to pray five times a day," I challenged her.

"That's true. But think about it, Coumba. These women are prostitutes. Now, it's not my place to say—because God will decide when they die whether they should enter paradise—but their chances are not very good. If they don't leave prostitution, he may not forgive them."

"But they ask for his forgiveness daily," I pointed out.

"So do I, Coumba," Maria retorted. "So do I."

WOMEN ARE ONE STEP BELOW

A few days before hundreds of thousands of Senegalese made their annual pilgrimage to the city of Touba to celebrate the return of the beloved holy leader Amadou Bamba after his exile in France, I heard that many of the prostitutes were traveling there as well. I pictured them praying at the mosque. When Maria explained that the prostitutes were going to seek clients among the pilgrims, I laughed at my assumption. "All work and no pray," I mused.

I asked Maria if the prostitutes had a source for condoms in or near Touba. "Not really," was her response. Because Touba was a holy city, products associated with sin, such as alcohol, cigarettes, xessal, mesh, and condoms, were banned. The prostitutes also were banned from the town a few years ago because they brought too much attention to themselves by dancing and singing late into the night. Now they had to find lodging outside city limits and wait for clients to go to them.

I assumed that the clinic furnished the women with extra condoms for the trip, as their number of clients skyrocketed. Hundreds of clients would visit them during the week, yet they had no access to additional condoms. "No," Maria informed me. "We can' t play favorites. Everyone, traveling or not, gets the same amount." I asked about the danger this posed to the women who had to buy expensive condoms or go without. She shrugged. I shook my head from side to side the way Aissatou did when recalling her husband's premature death.

I left the clinic and drove to Ndangane to return a registration card to one of the women. The laboratory results had just come in and showed that her previous STD was cured. She was not in her hut, so I gave it to Khady for safe keeping. "Business is slow," Khady complained as we sat on her bed. Senegal was hosting the international Africa Cup soccer matches, which kept men at home or in restaurants, glued to television sets. In-town prostitutes were scarce as well, as their families expected them to prepare for and take part in the pre- and post-game festivities. The Ndangane women did not have anywhere to go to join in the festivities. They sat in their huts frustrated that they would have to wait until that night's game was over to make any money.

I asked if I could follow up on our discussion about religion. Khady nodded. Just then a barefoot boy came to the door and looked at us in silence. She removed a cloth covering a bright green bucket and handed the heavy bucket to the boy. It was nearly full of water containing over a dozen half-floating condoms. The women thought this was the best way to avoid contact with the condoms' contents and ensure they would not be re-used. The boy struggled out the door, carried the bucket to an open area a block from the huts and emptied it. When he returned with the bucket a few minutes later she paid him.

"Do you ever go to the mosque?" I asked her.

"Sometimes."

"Do you think people can tell you're a prostitute?"

"At the market place it feels like they can. I feel them looking at me, looking down on me."

"Have they ever said anything to you?"

"No, not at the market place. But the neighbors here yell mean things at us all the time," she gestured toward the residential area across the way.

"And what about at the mosque?"

"Well, you know. 'Prostitute' isn't tattooed on my forehead. If I put on a *boubou*, cover my head with a scarf, and wear a veil over my face I can go to the mosque or to Touba without problem."

A client swept away the cloth hanging in the doorway and asked if she was available. She flashed me a plaintive smile, and I shook her hand goodbye, thanking her for her time. I left Ndangane and drove home, passing the big mosque, crossing over the train tracks, negotiating narrow dirt roads, and swerving around stray goats. I honked at pigs wallowing in mud from the last rain. I waved at people I had never talked to and they waved back, some shouting "Coumba!" or maybe it was "*Toubab!*" The words sounded alike and both described me. When I turned the corner, I was expecting the usual afternoon lull in activity on the road bordering pastel stucco houses with dirt front yards. Instead, the street was crowded with men and boys apparently returning from the small mosque a few blocks away. The mood was angry and excited, not reverent as usual. I looked at my watch; it was too early for the five o'clock prayer. Little Malick ran to me through the crowd and hopped in the car. But the streets were so crowded we had no place to go on our joy ride, to which I had been looking forward all day.

Mbodj explained that neighbors caught a man trying to steal the mosque's loud speaker. My first thought was that he was as tired of the loud call to prayer every morning at four forty-five as I was. In fact, no one knew what his motivation was, but they were clearly motivated to punish him for his crime. They locked him in the mosque while they debated his fate.

"He should be executed!" shouted an angry observer.

"The *grand marabout* should decide," reasoned another.

"I'll beat him up myself!" Mbodj declared.

"I'll go tell my dad!" Malick yelled in a high, squeaky voice, and disappeared into the crowd.

I asked Mbodj for the house key then walked to the kitchen and poured myself some cold bottled water. He walked to the outside of the kitchen and talked to me through the screen. "The phone rang three times today," he said. "Long rings. I think it was Michael." I put a handful of ice into a bowl and took it out to him. He was wearing a wool ski-cap, baggy "baby catcher" pants, and a red golf shirt with a white Jack Nicklaus insignia over the left breast—a gift from Michael.

"OK, I'll call him. He's coming down in a few weeks."

"Oh, good. Tell my boss I want to talk to him."

"Your boss?" I questioned with a smile. "Who pays you? Who feeds you? Who gave you an advance to build your second wife a hut? Who gave you a horse?"

He smiled but did not answer. I chalked up one for Islam and walked back into the house. Maria's quote from the Koran an hour earlier echoed in my head, "Men stand a step above women." This was the first time I managed a household and employed someone who looked to me for salary, tasks, and vacation time. I was proud that it was going well, despite my weakness for doling out money to Mbodj and others whenever they asked. Mbodj's insistence on regarding a man as his boss was not surprising, but frustrating. Interestingly, Michael's female cook always greeted me at the door, relieved *her* "boss" was home. She would then ask me to mediate between her and Michael, inferring that he was more likely to comply with her requests if they came from me.

I finished my water then walked around the corner to see Youma, my friend and Wolof tutor. She had gotten married a few days earlier and invited me to join in the celebration and take photographs. Because she married a relative she had known since childhood, the negotiations were quick because her family knew about his family and character. To speed up the process even more, her new husband "stole" her the night before by sneaking into her room. He told her younger siblings to sleep elsewhere, then had sexual intercourse with her.

It was her first time. In the morning, word spread quickly that the couple had consummated their marriage.

Youma's aunt was the first to talk with her. She asked for Youma's bed sheet, stained with blood. It was proof that Youma, twenty-two years old, had been a respectable Muslim girl and was a virgin. Then her mother visited her, followed by other elder female relatives and Youma's peers. The new bride was not permitted to go outside for a week, so stayed in bed. She relieved herself in a pot brought to her room by one of her younger sisters, Maguette.

Amid all the excitement and mystery we had no time for our usual talks. When I went to see her she was alone, but not for long. Before we could finish our greetings some of her friends burst into the room, laughing and boisterous. "Who's the *toubab*?" asked one. Annoyed at the expression originally used in reference to French colonists, Youma corrected her. "She's Coumba." I sat on the edge of her bed and held her hand as she chatted with her friends. I did not understand all that they said because they spoke rapidly in Wolof, but I heard *toubab* a couple times. Eventually the friends went outside to make some tea. Youma turned to me and smiled weakly. She was overwhelmed and in physical pain.

She said she was happy to be married, yet dizzy because it happened so quickly. She had never really considered marrying this man, but he was her father's sister's son, educated and hard-working. His first wife had recently left him when he refused to move with her to Switzerland, where she was offered a job. Wanting another wife to care for him and his son immediately, he chose Youma, a beautiful, smart, and responsible young woman.

"Will you be polygamous or monogamous?" I asked.

"Monogamous, I think."

"What about school?" She had a year left.

"I'll finish this semester, then I'll move to Dakar and go to school there."

"Can I get you anything?" I asked, looking absently at the Sylvester Stallone and Prince Charles posters on sky blue walls. She sat up a little, wiped some sleep from her dark brown eyes, and straightened her hundreds of tiny black braids decorated with a rainbow of beads. She grimaced as she moved, her strong white teeth brightening her face.

"Could you get your camera and take some photos of my friends?"

"Sure."

I went home for my camera. When I returned the women had gathered outside in the compound's courtyard so I could take a group shot. The woman who kept referring to me as *toubab* told me to take a picture of the change in Youma's body. The request surprised me. Although I was not sure of the purpose or intended subject matter, I said it would be impossible without a flash. After taking a few more group and individual photographs I said my goodbyes and left the compound, closing the large metal gate behind me, much to the dismay of little Malick and a neighborhood goat—the first hoping for a glimpse of the celebration and the second hoping for a scrap of food.

On the way home I saw one of Youma's childhood friends, also named Malick. A tall, confident, clean-cut man in his early twenties, he always asked how I was, where Michael was, where my mother was, and whether I had news from the United States. He also patiently answered my many questions. I said I was confused about Youma's situation. Malick explained that by stealing her, her husband avoided weeks of exchange between the families. He was also showing consideration for Youma's parents by keeping his plans a secret; if they had known what was taking place in their daughter's room across the compound they would have stayed up late worrying and wondering if she was a virgin.

Big Malick explained that because evidence showed that Youma was a virgin, the *griots* (praise singers) had come to sing praises of Youma and her family, who had raised her well. "I have never seen such a celebration," he said. "Her parents must have been proud. These days, girls aren't as likely to save themselves until marriage." Young men, he said, are rarely virgins at marriage. With whom are they having sex? Some women become "little prostitutes," having intercourse with young men who want to be sexually active but want to "spare" girls saving themselves for marriage. Sometimes, he said, a man might promise to marry the woman whose virginity took and together they lie about her status on their wedding night. It is common for such couples to pour goat blood on their bed sheets before inspection.

Still, the Wolof word *sey* was used for both intercourse and marriage, apparently because they were expected to happen simultaneously. If Youma had not been a virgin, her ashamed parents would not have been surprised if her fiance called off the marriage.

"Why does she have to stay in bed?" I asked Malick.

"She's weak. Plus, women walk in an ugly manner after losing their virginity." He took a bow-legged stance and put his arms out, as if trying to balance himself. "It's best for her to stay in her room until she's healed. Virgin girls and men shouldn't see her in this state."

A few days later, I went to Youma's compound for the family's usual Monday night viewing of their favorite show, "Dynasty," on their small black and white television. We were joined by dozens of neighbors who did not have electricity, let alone televisions. I was glad it was not raining, or we would have had to crowd into her parents' room. Outside, despite my polite objections, her father always insisted I take one of the two large armchairs placed on the decaying cement block surrounded by dirt. He sat in the other, under the dark sky, front and center with a perfect view of the television propped on a table. I beckoned Youma's five-year-old sister Maguette to sit on my lap. She welcomed the attention and opportunity to be hugged, as did I, and ignored her older siblings as they teased her for acting like a little girl. She should be sitting on the hard concrete or dusty ground with the rest of the children, they said, to help keep the goats and chickens away during the show. But Maguette stayed with me, watching rich *toubabs* whose dubbed French she barely understood.

The irony of watching a program about America's wealthiest people while sitting under African skies always amazed me. The story lines seemed far-fetched from the standpoint of someone living hand-to-mouth, but the Senegalese watched with interest as children were kidnapped for ransom, people received organ transplants in their own hospital suites, and families of four played on ranches large enough to house our entire neighborhood. When one couple had a wedding in their family's mansion Youma's father was in awe: "What a beautiful hotel!"

I said my goodbyes and walked home in the dark by the beam of my flashlight. I said good night to Mbodj and went into my bedroom to change when I heard footsteps in the living room. Peeking around the corner, I was relieved to see it was Youma. We laughed as I explained I thought someone was coming to kidnap me. We sat down at my dining room table and she showed me a blue plastic bag. These bags were so common—littering the ground and blowing into trees and bushes—that embassy employees referred to them as the national flower. Youma emptied the contents onto the table: an Italian pornographic magazine and several types of contraceptives. She asked what I thought would be the best method for her. I explained it would be better for her to go to the family planning clinic, but that she should be aware of the differences between condoms and contraceptives that do not prevent HIV and STD transmission. I asked if she had talked to her mother about it. "Mothers and daughters don't talk about that kind of thing," she said matter-of-factly. As we talked, she thumbed through the magazine, loaned to her by a married friend. She examined each photograph with intellectual curiosity. When she reached the advertisements at the end she asked if she could ride with me to the clinic in the morning. I agreed and she walked to the door, blue bag in hand.

"Let's have a peaceful night," she said.

"Peace only," I responded.

That night I reflected about the role of sex and sexuality in Senegalese women's lives. Prostitutes and non-prostitutes alike had strong moral rules to comply with, from those surrounding courting and marriage, which were closely monitored by parents, relatives and communities, to those beyond marriage and behind closed doors, which they believed were between only them and God. Youma was most concerned with the public repercussions of her behaviors, believing that if her family and others they were proud of her and regarded her as a responsible and devout young woman, God would be equally accepting.

In contrast, the prostitutes prayed to God for forgiveness for actions that their families, friends and communities would disdain if they knew about them. The prostitutes believed God would be more forgiving than mortals in some ways, for he could see the bigger picture, could judge them based on all their actions, not just the sinful ones. They rationalized that because they were good Muslims, whether in religious actions or merely in spirit, God would forgive them for engaging in shameful sexual practices because the practices enabled them to act responsibly in other aspects of their lives.

Similarly, Youma tried to act responsibly in her new role as wife, balancing her respect for tradition with her knowledge of modern concepts surrounding sex and personal health. Although Muslims believe that God has ultimate power over people's health and destiny, she and others still took measures to protect themselves, whether from conception or illness. Because of this, it is as necessary to understand concepts about destiny as it is to examine health and illness beliefs, some of which have direct ties to religious tenets. To this end, the following chapter focuses on Senegalese health beliefs and the ways in which Senegalese perceive traditional medicine and modern medicine in the era of AIDS.

5

Wolof Medicine and White Person Medicine

Youma was more educated about AIDS, contraception, and health care than most Senegalese women. This was due in part to her formal education, but was primarily the result of her close relationship with her late father, a respected nurse known throughout Kaolack. When he died, his brother took her mother as a third wife and moved in with her and Youma's three siblings, as was common. Her father's other wife, an older woman, remained in the household but did not marry Youma's new father. Youma was charged with caring for her aging step mother, who suffered from acute arthritis and high blood pressure. In this way, Youma learned about traditional and Western medicine.

When she had a persistent headache, Youma walked to her local *marabout*. He would say a prayer and tie a thin cloth around her head. Then he would grind up dried leaves and dissolve them in hot water. Sometimes, when he had aspirin in supply, he would crush a couple tablets into a powder and mix it in without telling her. When she did not feel like going to the *marabout*, Youma would ask me for aspirin.

Like Youma, many of my neighbors came to my door asking for medicine. When rubbing alcohol, peroxide, aspirin, vitamins, or band-aids seemed appropriate, I gave them out in small amounts. When the illness seemed more serious, I usually offered to take the person to the clinic.

Malaria was common during the mosquito-infested rainy season, so I took Youma's relatives to the clinic for medicine when they fell ill. Still, while malaria was a serious concern to me, they viewed it more as a seasonal flu. For protection, I took anti-malaria medication weekly and sprayed myself with mosquito repellent daily; they took few preventative measures. The main reason I feared getting sick was the clinic's reliance on injections to cure malaria and other illnesses, even when supplies were low and needles had to be re-used. The Senegalese belief that the best way to cure an illness is through injection reflects the French emphasis on introducing medication directly into the bloodstream, said the clinic doctor.

THE WHITE PERSON AND WOLOF MEDICINE

Late one night I was feeling very nauseous and hot. Hoping to cool off, I went into the back yard for some fresh air, and yelled out to Mbodj so he would not mistake me for a thief and shoot me with his hand-made bow and arrow. He had been asleep in his room and came staggering out, armed and rubbing his eyes. I said I did not feel well and sat down on the back step. He sat down on the ground nearby and asked my symptoms. I told him I felt like I was going to vomit. He guessed that I had malaria from the insect repellent I sprayed in my room and said he would fetch some *rat*, a local Senegalese plant, from Youma's father and make me some tea in the morning. I stayed a few more minutes, enjoying the night breeze on my face and the complete silence of the dark. With no street lights and few households that could afford electricity, the stars shone brightly. He went returned to his room adjoining the house and I went back into my room.

After tossing and turning for hours I felt myself finally float off to sleep. Just as the sun cracked the darkness Mbodj came to my window and woke me up.

"How are you Coumba? Have you slept?"

"I'm sleeping now."

"Good. Are you still sick?"

"Yes."

"Well, I'm on my way to Youma's to get some *rat*. Go back to sleep." I went back to sleep.

"Coumba?" he said five minutes later. "I am making you *rat* tea. Are you still asleep?"

"Yes."

"Well, when you wake up come outside and I will give it to you."

Unable to go back to sleep I went outside, barefoot, in a tee shirt and long shorts. I asked if he saw Youma, and he said that he had told her of my illness, which she diagnosed as lovesickness. He gave me a Styrofoam cup of cloudy, bitter tea. I drank it down. While I waited for relief from my symptoms I squinted from the brightness of day, wishing I could curl up with a good newspaper by a warm fire in a snow-covered mountain cabin. Suddenly I felt a wave of nausea. I ran into the house and reached the toilet just in time to vomit.

I walked slowly outside, unimpressed with Mbodj's medicine.

"It didn't work," I complained.

"Did you vomit?"

I nodded, cringing.

"It did work, Coumba! You're supposed to vomit. Now you've gotten rid of the bad thing that made you sick."

That made sense. Growing up with Western medicine, it had not occurred to me that alleviating symptoms did not eliminate their cause. As I thought about the differences, I realized I no long felt nauseous.

Still weak, I changed into a calf-length dress and drove to Ndangane to keep an appointment with Khady. Mbodj came along in case I felt ill again. He did not know how to drive, but having him with me made me feel better and gave him a chance to get away from the neighborhood. He asked the guard across the road to keep an eye on the house, promising him a pack of matches upon our return. Once in Ndangane I parked in my usual spot. I asked Mbodj if he wanted to come with me while I told Khady I could not stay. He declined, preferring to stay in the car. He was uncomfortable in the prostitutes' work place and looked around carefully, as if to see if there was anyone who would recognize him.

I found Khady in her hut and told her I was sick, but feeling better since I drank some *rat* tea.

"You took Wolof medicine (*garabu Wolof*)?" she asked, amused.

"Yes, my guard gave it to me. It worked."

"Of course it worked. Now you're a true Senegalese, Coumba. Most white people will only take white people medicine (*garabu toubab*)."

Rhama walked over to greet me.

"Coumba drank *rat*," Khady smiled.

"Good for you, Coumba," Rhama joined in.

They, like Youma, diagnosed my illness as lovesickness. I laughed weakly and said goodbye. Mbodj and I stopped by the magazine store for a week-old International Herald Tribune then went to the town's only grocery store, the size of an American 7-Eleven. I greeted three disabled men soliciting alms and gave money to one of them, who knew to share it with his companions. I told Mbodj to pick out something for himself while I stocked up on canned fruit juice. He joined me at the counter with coffee, sugar, and a box of matches, and I paid the Lebanese owner.

When we returned to the house, I called my friend Elizabeth, a teacher at a missionary school in Dakar. She comforted me, diagnosed my illness as the twenty-four-hour flu, and said she would pray for me. We hung up and I read the paper until I fell asleep for the rest of the day. The next day I thanked Mbodj for curing me. "We're all in it together," he grinned.

There were also times when I cured Mbodj of his illnesses. He would come to my kitchen window and wait until I looked out at him. "Coumba, you will give me something for my leg. It is sore." I gave him some aspirin. "Coumba, you will give me something for energy. I can barely sweep the patio." All I had was One-A-Day Plus Iron vitamins for women, so I gave him a week's supply. Most of my remedies worked, except for the prunes I gave to Youma's father when he complained of weeks of constipation. He was eventually cured by a *marabout*.

THE HEALTH BELIEF SYSTEM IN SENEGAL

The value of good health was evidenced in the daily conversations of the Senegalese. Common greeting questions included, "Is your body in peace?" (*sa yaram jamm?*) and "Isn't it that anyone (in your household) is sick?" (*mbaa kenn tawaatul?*). When asked what was most important in life, people always told me that good health was the most important factor. Next in line were food and money.

Through my discussions with prostitutes, clinic staff, neighbors, and other informants about health and illness I found that they grouped illnesses according to three distinct categories: cause, symptoms, and treatment (Frake 1961; Kleinman 1978; Spradley 1972; Yoder 1980). The Senegalese believed that illness, like most other factors in their lives, was caused by outside forces. They would say "an illness got someone" (*feebar mo ko japp*), rather than saying the person "got the illness." The force causing the illness was God, whether directly or indirectly. Many people said God gave AIDS to people to punish them. As Khady said, evil people suffer long and painful deaths, AIDS being the longest and most painful.

ORIGINS OF ILLNESS

Illnesses caused by devils (*deme*) or *marabouts* were regarded as God's work because he created these people and gave them free will. According to the women, neither a *deme* nor a *marabout* could give a person AIDS. Although the women did not articulate why this was the case, they gave detailed accounts of how an exchange of body fluids is necessary to disease transmission. So, as Khady pointed out, "you *can* get AIDS from a *marabout* or *deme*, but only if you sleep with one who is seropositive." Usually, however, *marabouts* and *demes* were more likely to cause illness from a distance.

Prostitutes and others knowledgeable about transmission tended to group AIDS with inherited conditions because they knew that a baby could "inherit" HIV from an infected mother. Khady believed that leprosy, for example, would be inherited by a child if either parent were a leper. Likewise, being a *deme* was viewed as an inherited state, passed from a mother to her children.

In the eyes of the prostitutes, AIDS was most similar to STDs because both were most commonly transmitted through sexual intercourse. Although they knew other behaviors could lead to HIV transmission, unprotected sexual intercourse was their biggest concern. In fact, the women called AIDS and other STDs *feebaru goor*, illnesses of men. The explanation was simple, they said: men gave STDs and AIDS to women. Using similar logic, men usually referred to STDs as *feebaru jigeen*, illnesses of women. The clinic doctor said the former term was more common because STD symptoms were more easily detected among men than among women, who could harbor a disease for months without knowing it. The longer an STD goes unchecked, the more likely it is to cause long-term health problems, such as sterility and ulcers, which increase the likelihood of HIV transmission by bleeding during intercourse.

Another contagious disease the women associated with AIDS was malaria. Knowing that both are found in the blood, the women reasoned that a mosquito could carry the virus from one person to another. Studies, however, have shown this is impossible (Mboup 1992). Similarly, the women linked AIDS with easily transmitted conditions like flues and colds, viewing saliva as a body fluid containing the virus. They worried they would catch HIV just breathing the same air as an infected person. Although no cases of infection were traced to this mode of transmission, convincing them otherwise would be difficult if not impossible.

SYMPTOMS OF ILLNESS

According to informants, symptoms of an illness gave an indication of its cause. The clinic doctor distinguished STDs by their physical manifestations. For example, he listed separately those that cause sterility, those that cause discharge, and those that cause sores. He placed diseases with two or more of these symptoms in each appropriate category. According to him, the general population's attempts to categorize AIDS resulted in mass confusion. It is an STD based on the most common form of transmission, but its symptoms are not the same as those of other STDs.

The doctor was also concerned the lack of symptoms during early stages of HIV infection might lead some to think they were not infected because they felt healthy. Looking healthy was also important, and heavy women were held to be healthy, happy, and more attractive to men. In contrast, thin

women were held to be undernourished physically and emotionally, thin from worry. While this belief existed well before
the advent of AIDS, the significance of thinness took on a life
of its own when AIDS entered the scene. Hearing that people
with AIDS lose weight as their immune systems deteriorate
and they succumb to opportunistic infections, the Senegalese
associated low body weight with AIDS. In fact, not only did
many prostitutes suspect thin individuals were infected, they
believed they could avoid infection by steering clear of thin
partners. They also believed thin people were more suscepti-
ble to HIV infection and rejoiced each time the clinic scales
showed they had gained weight.

TYPES OF TREATMENT

Treatment not only followed diagnosis, but it also figured
into the Senegalese classification of illnesses. In addition to
self-treatment and treatment by family members, the two main
sources of treatment were medical doctors and *marabouts*. The
latter term refers both to religious men who claim to have healing powers and to traditional healers who do not incorporate
religion into their practice. Because of widespread use of this
blanket term by informants, it was often difficult to differentiate
between the two types of healers.

Due to the lack of a cure for AIDS, people familiar with
AIDS compared it to heart disease, cancer, and tuberculosis,
all incurable for many years. Prostitutes said that, although
there was no cure, Western-educated doctors could probably
relieve more symptoms than *marabouts* could. This classification separated AIDS from many ailments that the women
were certain *marabouts* could cure, such as STDs, headaches,
infertility, and prolonged menstruation.

Still, many *marabouts* claimed they could cure AIDS.
Khady's *marabout* showed me some plant roots he said cured
an AIDS patient at the hospital where doctors had no success

alleviating his symptoms. The gravest danger of such stories is that people might begin to believe AIDS is curable and take fewer precautions (Schoepf 1992).

Despite their knowledge, the women said that if they were HIV positive they would try every treatment they could find. The clinic doctor was concerned about people seeking cures from *marabouts*, but acknowledged that belief in a cure could have psychological advantages. Hope can make a person feel better, he said. On the other hand, he and other Senegalese doctors rarely told HIV positive patients about AZT and other possibly life-prolonging drugs because the vast majority of Senegalese simply could not afford them. As with cancer and polio before it, the doctors of AIDS patients often preferred not to tell them their health status because a positive diagnosis was viewed as akin to a death sentence.

The stigma of AIDS in Senegal was so strong that people were reluctant to talk about it lest others think they were infected. They also feared discussing it would make it more of a reality. In essence, ignorance is bliss. One of the embassy drivers told me that people did not want to think about the possibility of being infected. "It's like cutting your finger. If you look away and don't see the blood, it won't hurt as much. With AIDS, if you don't know you're infected, you will suffer less."

DECISIONS ABOUT TREATMENT

The Senegalese I spoke with went through a number of phases when deciding how to treat an ailment. There were three spheres that they considered: the home, the *marabout*, and the doctor's office. Ailing individuals did all they could to treat an illness before seeking professional assistance. They relied on their own or a relative's knowledge of the variety of treatments available through the market and tried them first. If treatment was unsuccessful, they would most likely go to a nearby *marabout*. If his attempts failed, they would go to the hospital or dispensary.

Among the prostitutes, STDs were the most common conditions for which medical attention was sought. As did the majority of Senegalese, prostitutes first attempted to cure themselves. When they attended the clinic for semimonthly examinations, they tried to hide their symptoms from clinic staff. They were known to lie about vaginal lesions, saying they cut themselves shaving; anything to avoid a STD diagnosis and temporary loss of their registration cards. Non-prostitutes were also reluctant to seek STD treatment, mainly due to the fear of stigmatization. They would rather treat themselves or pray to be cured than be seen at the STD clinic sharing a bench with prostitutes. Belief in *marabouts'* ability to cure STDs is potentially dangerous due to traditional medicine's inability to rid the body of the bacteria causing the illness. While the medicine might alleviate the symptoms, the STD will proceed to secondary and more serious stages if undetected.

According to informants, *marabouts* could cure other illnesses, such as those caused by other *marabouts*. Khady said that *marabouts* could render doctors "blind" to the illness' cause, preventing diagnosis and treatment. In addition, *marabouts* were often more successful than doctors in curing illnesses for which one would go to a doctor first. For example, Fatou claimed she took the clinic's medicine for several weeks to end prolonged menstrual bleeding, to no avail. She finally visited Khady's *marabout*, whose medicine cured her within days. Relieved to have her registration card back, Fatou paid the *marabout* more than he charged and referred several patients to him. Khady said she was very hesitant to refer prostitutes to him since they were often unreliable, avoiding payment and jeopardizing her relationship with him.

In addition to their healing powers, *marabouts* were believed to have the power to cause illnesses. *Marabouts*, said informants, knew that if they used their powers to harm others they might be punished by God before or after their death. In a country where money was second only to health on people's lists of what was important, many *marabouts* were willing to fulfill the wishes of paying clients. Although many people said they did not think it was right for *marabouts* to use their powers to cause evil, they said they would pay for such assistance if necessary.

TRADITIONS WITH HEALTH IMPLICATIONS

An example of the marriage of traditional and Islamic religion that has medical implications is the perpetuation of certain ceremonies, some of which were practiced by ethnic groups prior to the introduction of Islam. Many of the people I interviewed reported widespread belief that male circumcision was required by Islam, but evidence suggests it was practiced by all ethnic groups regardless of religion. Other activities associated with rites of passage, such as tattooing, scarification, and female circumcision were still practiced by most ethnic groups. In addition to inherent health concerns, the re-use of instruments for these practices posed a high risk for HIV transmission. The clinic doctor said that educated *marabouts* and others who performed the procedures were aware of the need to sterilize or dispose of used instruments. This was not always possible, however, due to lack of sterilization materials. Most people would rather re-use instruments than postpone a ceremony.

Although evidence is inconclusive, several theories have developed regarding the effects of male and female circumcision on HIV transmission. For example, male circumcision might correlate with lower rates of HIV by inhibiting infection in men (Bongaarts et al. 1989; Kreiss and Hopkins 1993). In contrast, some sources suggest female circumcision could increase transmission because of bleeding caused by tearing of scar tissue during intercourse (Mboup 1992). There is a growing movement to prevent female circumcision because of the

long-term health and psychological problems it causes. Such
traumatic surgery is extremely painful for young girls, who
usually undergo it at puberty. Years later, the women can suffer from incontinence, sterility, and pain during intercourse
and childbirth (Gueye 1992; Messing 1990). Among the one
hundred women I interviewed, fifteen had undergone some
form of circumcision (the Wolof term *xanaaf* is used for all
forms, including male circumcision).

Another painful and potentially harmful procedure is tattooing. Fulbe women who grew up in the 1930's and 40's were
tattooed around the outside of their mouths. As with most
puberty rites, girls were to show their courage and ability to
endure pain. This type of tattoo was also considered attractive
by men. But, eventually esthetics changed, and the practice di-
minished. Tattooing gums remained popular, though not as a
rite of passage. Fatou said people of all ages and ethnic groups
tattooed the area above and below their teeth with powder from
roasted peanuts to enhance the whiteness of teeth and prevent
gum disease. Fatou had her gums tattooed during her first
pregnancy to spare her unborn child the need to undergo the
procedure. The clinic's dentist said there was no scientific evidence that tattooing was healthful despite claims that the char-
coal injected into the gums has hygienic properties. On the
contrary, he said that it was often a source of infection.

Another tradition with potentially negative health implications is scarification, most common among men and women
going through puberty. Toucouleur and Bambara women
were most likely to receive facial scars, usually in the form of
small lines next to their eyes. The popularity of this and other
practices could present a health risk if instruments were
shared. Because people did not attach ritual significance to the
sharing of instruments, the problem of re-use was an economic, rather than a cultural, one.

In contrast to these practices that are potentially harmful,
other beliefs and behaviors were held to preserve people's

health and well-being. For example, people believed they should not travel on Tuesdays, Wednesdays, and Fridays because accidents were likely to happen. Rhama said if something went wrong during travel on those days, one's luck would remain bad. According to local lore, a group of women closed themselves in a hut on a Tuesday and set fire to it when their husbands did not return from an inter-ethnic war (Carr 1985). From then on, Tuesday was regarded as a day on which bad things happen as the result of leaving home. Mbodj said that the prophet Mohammed died on Wednesday, since regarded as a day of bad luck. Friday was also seen as a bad day for travel because what one does on a Friday continues, meaning one might continue going and not return. On the other hand, Friday was seen as a good day to make a large sum of money, to have a child, or to buy cloth for carrying a child on one's back since one would like these events to continue happening.

Mbodj told me he did not usually comply with travel taboos because he did not want them to interrupt his life. Shortly after our discussion, he left Kaolack on a Wednesday to return home to the bush. He walked to the public transport station and paid to ride about forty miles on a horse cart, slower but much less expensive than a taxi or bus. About half way down there the cart suddenly lost its front right wheel. Passengers, baggage, and livestock flew in all directions. Mbodj hit the ground head first and suffered from a long, deep cut on his forehead above his right eye. He jumped up to check on the other passengers, including several women, one of whom was pregnant. They were bruised and upset, but not seriously injured. While the driver fixed the wheel, Mbodj ran around the countryside rounding up sheep and goats that escaped during the excitement. When Mbodj returned to Kaolack he told me the story then announced he would not travel on a Wednesday for a while.

In part because of the taboo, I decided to travel to Dakar on a Wednesday, knowing traffic would be light. It had been two

months since I spent time away from Kaolack and I was growing cynical about the scarcity of health care supplies and the
complexity of life for Senegalese women. I knew I could not
change the culture, the system, the staff's attitudes, or the
prostitutes' lives, yet I was at a crossroads myself: should I
shrug my shoulders and accept it as a given or advocate
change? Needing time to analyze my reactions and regain perspective, I took a taxi from my house to the transport station,
switched to a bush taxi, and arrived in Dakar Wednesday
evening without incident.

Whereas this chapter has analyzed the role of tradition and
patterns in Senegalese life in terms of beliefs about illness prevention and treatment and actions that might adversely affect
health, the next chapter explores some people's efforts to get
away from aspects of their lives or surroundings. In my case,
a trip to Dakar was an attempt to escape frustration with the
ways in which traditional beliefs and practices, tempered by
social and economic constraints, affected the lives of the
women. The actions of others similarly represent attempts to
run away from concepts and environments that troubled
them. The reasons for and consequences of their flights vary,
but the act of running away, mentally or physically, is one I
found to be universal.

6

Running Away

She just abandoned herself.

—Khady (describing a colleague)

RUNNING FROM REALITY

I spent almost a week with Michael in Dakar, during which I picked up my mail, raided his kitchen cabinets for supplies, and relaxed on the beach at the westernmost tip of the African continent. When it was time to go, I packed my bag and dressed in Michael's red Nike tee shirt, my favorite jeans, and old canvas tennis shoes. Michael drove me to the bustling Dakar public transport station, where we quickly found a seven-seater bush taxi heading south. I squeezed between two large women in the last of the car's three rows, glad to be far from the windshield. I preferred not to watch the driver dodge horse carts, stray goats, pot holes, and villagers who did not look both ways before crossing the road. A couple of chickens and a goat were tied to the roof with the baggage, and I could hear their pleas for help as we drove along the stretch of four-lane highway that turned into a two-lane road a few miles out of town. Already feeling warm, I asked one of my neighbors to roll down her window. Not surprisingly, the handle was missing. Fortunately, a passenger in the row in front of us loaned us the one in his door.

When I arrived at my house Mbodj warned that there were two male Peace Corps volunteers in my house. "They insisted they were your friends," he said suspiciously, concerned I would be angry he did not send them away. I assured him it was not a problem and told him to put down his machete.

Inside, I was glad to see Mike and Mark, as the ride from Dakar usually left me feeling dusty and lonely. I had met them several months earlier when traveling in southern Senegal with my brother. Mike had just gotten out of the bath and Mark was listening to Cat Stevens on my miniature walk-man speakers. I made some spaghetti and we caught up on each others' news. I felt comforted to hear they were also facing the dilemma of accepting things as they are, fighting to change them, or running away from the confusion and pain they evoke. The men, both in their late twenties with matching long, brown hair and full beards said they were AWOL from the Peace Corps and heading to Dakar to quit their volunteer jobs. Both had been in-country several months, learned local languages, and did their best to find projects that would benefit the people in their assigned villages. When the projects did not get off the ground, their hopes of improving the villagers' lives seemed futile. This feeling of powerlessness was compounded by the encounters they had with their neighbors.

Mark had been in the Casamance region, known for its lush vegetation, rice paddies, and exotic animals, where he lived with the village chief and his family in their compound. He grew quite close to the children, especially a four-year-old girl who was fascinated with the *toubab*. Like the rest of us, he was tired of people yelling "*toubab, toubab!*" every time, it seemed, he stepped out of is hut. But he did not mind it from this little girl. Late one night her father called Mark to his hut, where the little girl lay seriously ill. Mark knelt down and realized she had stopped breathing. He gave her artificial resuscitation, to no avail. When she died the others in the hut with him communally shrugged. Mark walked outside and began to cry, feeling more useless than ever. The chief tried to comfort him. "Don't be sad," he said. "She was just a girl."

"That was the straw that broke the camel's back," Mark said. "I realized that although I have tried my best, I'm not going to help. I'm wasting my time living here, trying to save the world. There are other things I could be doing that wouldn't depress me so much."

Mike nodded. "I was sitting in my hut, reading *Zen and the Art of Motorcycle Maintenance* and this old villager walked in and began crying on my shoulder. He was upset because his 'true love' married another man and his heart was broken." Vaguely interested, Mike asked the man who the girl was. Hearing her name, Mike knew it was the fourteen-year-old in a neighboring compound.

"I mean, I had no sympathy for this guy. I was disgusted. Here he is, feeling sorry for himself. He's probably sixty years old and he has three wives. And he wants this teenager for himself. It was all I could do to politely tell him I was sorry, but that I wanted to be alone. Then I thought, if I'm going to spend all my time in my hut so I don't explode on one of the villagers, it's time to go."

Mike rode his moped to Mark's village and slept in his friend's hut on the bare dirt floor. The next day they left their mopeds behind and headed north in crowded buses along treacherous, pot-holed roads, stopping at the beach for several days to bask in the sun and plan their strategy for telling the Peace Corps Country Director they were leaving. After dinner we went into town for a drink. When we saw there were only a few people at a restaurant frequented by Peace

Corps volunteers, I suggested we go to a bar in Ndangane to observe the neighborhood at night.

I parked near the bars rather than near Khady's hut. With no street lights, the area was pitch black. We made our way from the car toward the light coming from one of the bars. A literal hole in the wall, the bar stood out only because of the hand-painted sign above the door: BAR AMBIANCE. The irony always made me smile.

"Hi Coumba," came a voice from the darkness as we approached.

"Hi," I said. "Who is that?"

"Astou," she replied. "You don't recognize your mother?"

"It's black," I said, trying to remember the Wolof word for dark. Astou laughed her sincere, motherly laugh and walked with us into the bar where I could see her better and introduce her to my friends. She was wearing a red, white, and blue *boubou* patterned after the American flag. Her left earlobe, torn from years of heavy earrings, was split from mid-lobe on down. She closed the gap with a band-aid, from which hung a large gold hoop earring matching the one in her other ear.

"I'm her mother," she told my friends, clasping her right breast with her right hand to signify maternity.

ASTOU

Astou was notorious in Ndangane. She claimed to be thirty-six years old, was really forty-nine, and looked about sixty. Her small, sunken face evoked both sadness and sympathy. She frequented the bars, drank often, and had been arrested dozens of times for disrupting the peace. She was one of the women Khady and Rhama referred to as the "drinkers" and she often went to Khady for financial and emotional support, saying she was her daughter. Khady, who like many of us was touched by Astou's sweet nature and intense vulnerability, helped her extensively over the years. Their relationship dated back to their time in Mauritania in the 1970's. "I'm the one who took her to the hospital when her finger turned green from infection. I held her other hand when they cut it off," said Khady. As proof, Astou showed me the stump. "I've bought her food, shoes, and clothes, I've given her condoms, paid for clinic fees, and bought her foot medicine (for arthritis). She's like a mother to me," added Khady.

Despite the assistance Khady provided Astou, she discouraged Astou's exploits. "She's going to die here. She's going to die a prostitute," Khady said sadly. Khady, Rhama, and other younger prostitutes were sure they would leave prostitution before they died. That was the hope of most of the women, but not the reality. Khady persistently tried to persuade Astou to live with her son, a military officer, and his wife in Dakar.

"I have no son," Astou insisted. "Only two daughters," she pointed to Khady and me.

"You told me in our first interview that you have two sons," I countered.

"Well, one of them is chasing women across the world and the other one and his wife don't like me. I'm better off without them and they're better off without me."

Khady said Astou, a famous dancer and radio singer in her heyday, did not like living with her son because he and his wife criticized her work as a prostitute and would not let her drink. He repeatedly invited her to live with him in peace, but by her own account she could not adapt to a sedentary and restricted lifestyle after more than twenty years as a prostitute. "I'm a chronic prostitute," said Astou. "I'm staying here until the black taxi (hearse) takes me away."

Other "drinkers" resisted similar invitations to move in with family. Ashamed of their drinking and participation in prostitution, they preferred to stay out of their families' lives rather than feel humiliated and risk humiliating them. As we sat down in the musky, dimly-lit Bar Ambiance I spotted several women who seemed to be running away from problems by drinking excessively. They were caught in a vicious cycle of going to bars to drink and meet clients, then accepting whatever clients would pay them so they could afford drinks. The women who drank regularly were less likely to insist on condom use due to indifference or inability to negotiate effectively after heavy drinking. Still, all the women with the exception of Astou said their clients always wore condoms.

Astou sat down with us at a wobbly metal table, proud to be in the bar with three *toubabs*. Several prostitutes greeted me and I introduced them to my friends, who spoke Pulaar and Diola to them. A few bought us drinks, and we reciprocated. As we drank, I watched the prostitutes interact with potential clients. The exchanges were friendly yet businesslike as they negotiated a fee and walked out of the bar. I turned around and noticed a man standing a few feet away trying to get our attention. With dramatic movements of his hands and arms, he began an impromptu magic show of sorts. He took a box of wooden matches out of his pocket and removed one. I thought he would make it disappear into thin air, but he held it at the opening of his right nostril instead. I leaned back, fearing he would light it. Instead, he inhaled and the match disappeared. We three *toubabs* looked at each other in disbelief. He took out another match, ready to convince us we had seen correctly. Astou, unfazed until she noticed our expressions, yelled at the magician. He looked dejected then trudged back to his table in the corner.

Just as we turned back to our drinks, another man who could barely stand started a conversation with me. His slurred speech was difficult to understand, so I did not know what to say. Sensing this, he began to dance, providing us with our second impromptu show of the night. Suddenly he stopped, turned around, and vomited on the floor. The bartender helped him outside while the cashier dumped a bucket of dirt over the vomit. We decided it was time to go, and stepped out into the darkness.

The contrast between night and day in Ndangane was just that: two different worlds. At night it was calmly quiet and almost pretty, the moon shining down on rows of thatch work huts, the stars bright from the absence of artificial light. The only ground light came from lanterns inside the women's huts. Nighttime illuminated the true nature of their profession. Each woman not seeking clients in one of the local bars sat quietly outside the door of her hut, fending for herself, hoping to attract clients and make money for food and her family. The women spoke little, preferring to absorb the stillness of the night, waiting for its end and the chance to return home.

As we walked along the dirt paths toward Khady's hut, I had trouble seeing. People passing us greeted me by name, but I had to stand very close to identify them. When we arrived at Khady's hut the door was closed, cracks of light shining through the walls. Assuming she had a client, we walked back to the car where I gave Astou some money, explaining it was for food, not cigarettes or drinks. She clasped her breast and gave me a hug. "She's my daughter," she told my friends again, then walked off into the darkness.

While heavier women were more successful during the day, thinner women attracted more clients at night. Khady and Rhama said this was due to men's perception that thinner women were younger. Unable to see the women's faces clearly at night, men chose those who appeared younger to avoid intercourse with older women even though most men preferred heavy women. "It's like having sex with my mother!" one man exclaimed when he saw Astou in the morning light. "All she has left is lips," commented another as a crowd gathered outside her hut when the client complained Astou refused to have sex with him after taking his money.

This was the type of exploit for which Astou was known. She tricked her clients into giving her money, then claimed they gave her less than they did, or that they gave her nothing at all. "That's not a good strategy for a prostitute!" Khady mused.

More often than not, the men walked away when a crowd formed, preferring to lose their money rather than fight with a woman with whom they no longer wanted to have intercourse anyway. On those occasions when the men were bent on getting their way, Astou was beaten, scratched, and arrested.

The morning after we visited Bar Ambiance, Mark and Mike loaded their bags in my car. As was typical, a group of curious neighborhood children congregated near my driveway. Earlier in the year such attention made me feel uncomfortable, especially when the young voices demanded cashew fruit from my tree and money from my pocket. I learned to flatly deny their requests unless I had enough fruit, used tennis balls, or candy to go around. But, because the crowds grew too big and the children pushed each other trying to get to the front, I decided it was more effective to offer gifts quietly to Malick and the children who lived next door.

But Mark still reacted negatively to the children's fascination with *toubabs*. "*Toubab, toubab!*" they cried. "Senegalese, Senegalese!" he yelled back. Amid the commotion Mike calmly asked me which child he could scare. Before I understood his question, he lunged at a small boy near him and roared like a lion. The boy broke into tears and, with the rest of the crowd, backed away to a safe distance. The act was angry and inappropriate, but a clear sign of the frustration an outsider feels when receiving unwanted attention. As we drove to town a pensive Mike said that an American friend asked him what it was like to be in the Peace Corps. "It's like putting on a bunny suit, going to the busiest intersection in New York City, and jumping up and down. When onlookers ask what you're doing, you say 'I'm here to save you!'."

I drove them to the transport station and watched them board a packed, beat-up bus headed for Dakar. Then I went to Ndangane to take Astou to the clinic. The arthritis in her left ankle was acting up, so she could barely walk. "She walks fine until you get here, Coumba," Khady confided. Still, Astou's foot was very swollen and tears were in her eyes. She said she could not go to the clinic because she did not have a *boubou* to put on, insisting her tee shirt and old *pagne* were not appropriate for a trip into town.

The night before, Astou slept on the dirt outside Bar Ambiance because another prostitute, Goundo, kicked her out of a hut Goundo rented her. This was punishment for angering the neighbors. According to Goundo and Khady, Astou heard drumming in the residential area and walked over to join in the festivities. While dancing with the women, Astou began to take off her clothes. The neighbors called the police, who took Astou away, beat her, then left her at Goundo's hut. Goundo knew that Astou's behavior would only exacerbate the women's relationship with the neighbors, so she kicked Astou out of the hut, which Astou used for work and sleep because she could not afford to rent a room. Goundo refused to give Astou her belongings, and Astou never saw her beloved American flag *boubou* again. Once a talented and respected performer, mother, and wife who turned to prostitution after she became too old to dance and her husband left her, Astou had sunk as low as she could get. "I would beg, but God wants me to do this," she said sadly of her more than fifteen years as a prostitute.

After listening to Astou's story, Sadio, the delegate who liked to visit government officials, took Astou into her hut and put a clean *boubou* on her. She then put a dark black wig over Astou's short, thinning hair and dabbed her with perfume. When Astou emerged, Khady and I told her she was beautiful. She smiled from the attention and climbed slowly into my car. As we drove through town to the clinic she began to cry. I reached out for her hand.

"Would you live with your son in Dakar if I drove you?" I asked.

"No. But I would go back to America with you."

I parked in front of the clinic and walked around the car to help Astou. Arm in arm, we walked up the steps and through

the doors to the head nurse's desk. I explained that Astou's
leg had worsened and asked for some medicine. The head
nurse looked up from her nail file, glanced at the leg, and said
it was no worse than usual. I asked if she minded if I had a
doctor look at it. She shrugged. I walked down the hall to the
office of the head of the dispensary and asked him to come by
the STD clinic when he could. He followed me back, examined Astou, and gave us a prescription. Throughout the visit,
Astou talked to the doctor and clinic staff about her aches and
pains, about being tired, about the police beating her. By the
time we were ready to go, her spirits were much improved
and her limp less pronounced. She walked over to Maria and
gave her some money for condoms.

"I'm not going to give you condoms," Maria snapped. "You
are sick and you haven't eaten all day. Go buy something to
eat."

"Forget the details and give me my condoms!" Astou shot
back.

Maria laughed in surprise at Astou's assertiveness and
handed her a bag of condoms. Astou lifted Sadio's *boubou* and
tucked them into her *pagne* then almost gingerly took my arm
and walked back to the car. We stopped at the market place,
where I bought her a couple of oranges, a baguette, and a
hard-boiled egg.

While Khady was my main informant, Astou was my main
concern. I knew I could not take her away from her difficult life
or alleviate the physical and mental pain she suffered, but I
made a point of showing I cared. Because Wolof was a second
language for both of us (she was raised speaking Pulaar), we
could not communicate well verbally, but our gestures and few
words conveyed our feelings of friendship and empathy. I always made a point of greeting her the way I did Couna, even
though she was not respected as an elder by the other women.
The other prostitutes did not seem bothered by this or my occasional gifts, as she was obviously the most desperate. They

knew she had few clients because of her tired appearance and age and that clients who did not mind her age knew of her tricks. When they went to her it was usually as a last resort.

When Michael and I visited Ndangane on a weekend, Astou invited Khady and us into the new hut Khady rented for her. Astou patted the bed, indicating we should sit down. She slowly lowered herself to the dirt floor then rummaged through her bucketful of belongings. She grabbed a handful of cowry shells and threw them onto the floor in front of her. Studying their placement, she was happy to see that Michael and I would marry and have two children. Khady nudged me and smiled. Typically, one would wish for and predict several children, the more the better. But Astou had heard me tell Khady I wanted one boy and one girl, so whenever she praised me she wished for me a happy life and two healthy children. This always drew reactions from others, who found it odd. Continuing her analysis of the shells, Astou commented that every time she threw them at least one shell landed on top of another. This meant, she said, that there was another person affecting my relationship with Michael. Khady nudged me again. Astou was right; we were both in the process of ending relationships we had in the United States.

The next time I saw Astou she was on her bed fending off an angry client with a chain the size of a bicycle lock. She had fresh scratches on her neck and chest. Khady and I pulled the slight man off Astou and Khady told him to leave. He said that he wanted to have intercourse with Astou despite her resistance. Khady, twice his size, looked down into his face and repeated her order. He left without a backward glance. Astou, unshaken, stood up, straightened her clothes, and thanked us.

GOUNDO

Violence was not alien to the prostitutes, especially those who drank or had serious emotional problems. Goundo, the tall, slender, and dark woman who withheld Astou's belongings as punishment for her drunken behavior, was known for loud and hostile outbursts, which grew worse after her fiancé left her. Prior to their break-up, the couple owned a successful boutique in Ndangane, and Goundo promised to quit prostitution after their marriage. But shortly before the wedding was to take place, a contingent of her fiancé's relatives traveled from their village to Kaolack and demanded that he return with them. They said they disapproved of his marriage to a prostitute, and insisted he marry a woman they had chosen for him.

"If he loved her he would have stayed," Khady commented. "But no one wants to marry a prostitute."

"But she said she was going to leave the profession."

"Once a prostitute, always a prostitute. You can get married and say you'll stop working, but if a man offers you money, it's very hard to refuse. Besides, your husband will not forget. Every time he gets mad at you he'll remind you that you were a prostitute."

Shortly after her fiancé left, Goundo "went crazy." She closed down the boutique and left Ndangane without her belongings. She went home to her family, who took her to the hospital. Several months later, Goundo returned to Ndangane claiming to be cured. "But she wasn't," Khady testified. "See how her skin is black? Her heart is also."

I soon saw this for myself. While I was interviewing Khady on one side of a row of huts, we heard Goundo screaming on the other side. She was fighting with Nafy, her younger and prettier neighbor. Before we could reach the corner Nafy emerged from behind the huts. Her forehead was bleeding and already swollen; Goundo had hit her in the head with a Coke bottle. According to Nafy, Goundo, jealous when Nafy agreed to spend the night with a client, attacked her.

Khady and I took Nafy to the clinic, where they gave her several stitches. I asked the social worker if he was planning to talk to Goundo. Ever timid, he said he would when he saw her next. I offered to drive him to Ndangane right then, but he declined.

Trying to convince him Goundo needed help, I told him of Goundo's recent punishment of Astou. He smiled calmly, not surprised. It was clear he did not plan to get involved. Whether or not it was his job to counsel the women, the women thought it was, and they needed someone who could mediate when they had disagreements, especially violent ones.

I walked Nafy to the car. She staggered along, due to the combination of injury and too many swigs of palm wine. "Thank you, Coumbis," she slurred, changing my name to show affection. Back in Ndangane, I helped her lie down in her hut then went to Khady's hut to talk with her and Amy. I told them it seemed the social worker would not talk to Goundo, so Amy said she would ask Ibra to mediate between the women. Just then Cire, a tall, strong woman came into the hut yelling.

"Tell Ndeye to keep her kids away from my hut!"

"Why?" Khady asked.

"They're looking through the cracks, trying to see me and my client!"

"OK, I will." Khady sighed. Cire stormed out.

"Some days it's so calm here. And some days it's too crazy." Khady sighed again, pulled herself up, and walked out the door.

NAFY

Nafy had not always been a drinker. Orphaned early in life, she married young and became a skilled seamstress. After three marriages and three children, she moved to Dakar with a man she hoped to marry. Her luck turned when a neighborhood man was murdered and the police suspected Nafy's boyfriend was responsible. When she heard they were looking for him, Nafy gave him money and told him to run away, certain he would not get a fair trial. Hours later, the police showed up at her door and threatened to beat her until she told them where her boyfriend was. Nafy refused to say a word. They took her to prison, where she stayed for over a year, reportedly receiving several shock treatments. Still, she would not speak. The treatments, her friends said, made Nafy crazy. "She just abandoned herself," Khady said simply.

When Nafy was finally set free, she was no longer the happy, confident woman her friends knew. She began drinking for comfort and, her vision impaired by cataracts, could not resume her work as a seamstress. She eventually turned to prostitution for income and moved to Kaolack, knowing she would never see her boyfriend again. She told me she drank and practiced prostitution because other prostitutes went to the *marabout* to put spells on her. And even though her children offered to take care of her, she cut all ties with them. She knew their support could provide her a way out, but she wanted to protect them from her sins. She also wanted to protect them from the AIDS virus, which she suspected she might have.

EVA

Unlike Nafy, Eva's plan was to return home should she fall ill. Although she was HIV positive, the symptoms that prevented her from working were due to advanced colon cancer. When she first became sick, the clinic staff sent her and another ill woman to the hospital in Dakar for treatment. The rumor was that the two women were HIV infected, but clinic staff had not told them their HIV status. Instead, staff said the women's symptoms would be better treated in Dakar, where the women's new doctor was expected to break the news to them. After a brief hospital stay and little attention, both women decided to return to their families' villages. Knowing Eva had no resources, her prostitute friends pooled enough money for her to go home.

When Eva arrived in her village with little money and no strength, her family and friends made it clear they did not want her there. For years they had not heard from her, had seen no money, had received no help in the fields during cultivation. Why should they help her now that she was dying? They put up with her but did not go out of their way to comfort or care for her. Like many families, they did not realize that she had kept her distance over the years to protect them from the stigma of being related to a prostitute.

When Eva gathered enough strength, she returned to Ndangane to resume her small palm wine business and begin practicing prostitution again. "It's ugly here," she said. "But now it feels more like home than my village." She bled every time she had intercourse and often refused to let clients wear condoms because the lubrication stung her open wounds. When they heard this, the clinic's head nurse, doctor, and social worker paid her a visit, only because they happened to be in Ndangane for the filming of a documentary about the clinic's AIDS program. The head nurse tried to talk Eva into handing over her registration card, but Eva argued she did not want to lose her income or her pride. Because her family was unwilling to support her, she would continue supporting herself until her death.

"But how much money do you need? Just enough for food. We'll help you with that," the head nurse argued.

"I need *boubous* too," Eva replied.

"All you need is two. One to wear while you wash the other."

"That's not enough. I can't wear the same thing every day. I can't take handouts for food."

The head nurse told Eva she would not validate her registration card after her next medical examination. In response, Eva did not go to the clinic again. True to her word, she worked until the night she died while sleeping in her work hut, too weak to walk to her rented room a block away.

Sparing one's family the stigma of prostitution and AIDS was common among the prostitutes. The difference between the drinkers and non-drinkers, however, was that the first tended to cut all ties with their families while the latter remained very close to theirs. Another difference was that the drinkers' families most likely knew of the women's activities, while the non-drinkers did all they could to hide them. Although the cause-effect relationship was not clear, nor was it the same in every case, it seemed that drinkers began drinking after their families learned of their work. In despair because they felt they had brought their families shame, they tried to numb their feelings with alcohol. For other women, drinking made it harder for them to conceal their activities. Further, because drinking was associated with prostitution, families might have guessed the women were prostitutes when they learned of their drinking. In any case, the more they drank, the less they cared about seeing their families, taking care of themselves, and leaving prostitution.

Khady and other non-drinkers agreed that once a family finds out a woman is a prostitute, it is difficult for any woman to go home. The last time Khady went home her teenage daughter acted strangely, barely speaking to her. This led Khady to suspect her daughter knew the truth. Khady stayed away longer than usual then decided she would rather talk to her daughter openly than risk losing her love and trust. After all, she pointed out, most prostitutes did this work to provide for their children.

OULI

But there were exceptions. While most women had children before becoming prostitutes, Ouli never had the chance to become close to four of her five children. Arguing that Ouli was an unfit mother, the children' s fathers raised them and forbade Ouli to visit. Her fifth, however, remained with her because his father initially did not want custody. Months later, he changed his mind and begged Ouli to give the boy, Semba, to him. Ouli told him it was too late, but admitted to others that caring for Semba was more than she could handle. Semba was usually nude save for a piece of worn cloth wrapped around him. When asked why, Ouli would claim she lost his clothes. Without someone to baby-sit, she took Semba everywhere, including to bars and hotels in town when she was looking for clients. Sometimes she left him in their rented room, asleep and unattended, while she looked for a client. Once she found one she would take him to her room, where they would have intercourse as the baby slept.

The first time I talked to Ouli she handed me Semba, a beautiful and pleasant eight-month-old boy. She maintained he would have a better life with me in the United States. Surprised, I asked Maria how serious the offer was.

"Very serious."

I talked with the clinic staff about Ouli's situation, and they said they would keep on eye on Ouli while encouraging her to keep Semba. A month later, Ouli rushed into the clinic with Semba in her arms. He was fine, but she was bleeding from wounds to her chest and back. She said she had gone to see Aicha, another prostitute who worked in town. Aicha was with her daughter, also a registered prostitute, when Ouli asked Aicha to repay her some money she loaned her. Aicha, angry, ordered her daughter to hold Ouli still. According to Ouli, Aicha took Semba and handed him to someone else, then pulled out a knife and stabbed Ouli several times. I was not at the clinic when Ouli and Semba arrived, but Maria described Ouli's injuries. "If you had been here you would have cried." They sent her to the hospital for stitches.

The clinic staff encouraged Ouli to press charges, but she preferred to "regulate" the problem herself to avoid provoking Aicha further. When it was time to have her stitches removed I took her to the hospital and held Semba in the waiting room while she was in with the doctor. Passers-by stopped to admire the handsome baby, probably curious about our relationship.

When I drove them home I could not believe my eyes. If Ndangane can be politely described as dirty, Ouli's neighborhood was simply filthy. There was trash everywhere, the roads were pure mud, and the open areas were covered with human waste and garbage. Blue plastic bags provided the only color, artificial flowers dotting uninhabitable swampy land.

Ouli invited me in and showed me around. She rented a room in a compound owned by a mother of three. No one was home except for a small puppy tied to a pole, starving for water, food, and attention. She forgot to feed him that morning. The compound itself was well-kept, with fresh laundry hanging across it, evidence of hours of labor by Ouli's landlord. With no well or water pump nearby, Ouli contributed to household chores by fetching water from a well two miles away. Each morning she carried Semba on her back, securing him with a cloth supporting his bottom and tied at her stomach. She trudged through the mud with her plastic bucket, filled it and returned, balancing it on her head.

Two months after offering me Semba, Ouli grew more desperate to give him away. She showed up at the head nurse's house on a Saturday night and begged her to take the baby, afraid she would harm him if she kept him a minute longer. The head nurse felt she had little choice, so took him for the rest of the weekend.

On Monday the clinic staff had a meeting and decided to take Semba to Ouli's mother in hope she would care for him. The head nurse and social worker asked me to drive, so we piled in and drove to a house near the large mosque a quarter mile across the train tracks from my house.

I held Semba while they talked to Ouli's big brother, who explained that their mother would return from Dakar the following evening, agreeing to take Semba in the meantime. Ouli sat by quietly, ambivalent about handing Semba over to a woman she hated. After holding Semba for a half hour, it was difficult to hand him to this man, a stranger to the child. But the new uncle took him gently and smiled. Semba had that effect on everybody.

As we walked to the car, Ouli started to cry. The head nurse and social worker were also wiping away tears. On the way to the clinic they told me Ouli's mother had beaten Ouli and her siblings and was rumored to be "crazy." Ouli left home at thirteen to live with her aunt until she was eighteen. Pregnant with her first child, Ouli moved into a rented room and started selling perfume and cloth in Ndangane. Aware that her prostitute clientele earned much more than she, she accepted one of many offers from would-be clients who noticed her walking through the prostitutes' work area. A very pretty, fair-skinned woman with scars next to each eye, Ouli soon found she could make a lucrative living from prostitution. When I asked if she ever practiced in Ndangane, she said she preferred meeting men in town and taking them to a hotel room or her own room.

"I can get better clients than the Ndangane women do. They are old. I am young. There is no reason for me to work there."

Although Ouli registered at the clinic and kept most of her scheduled medical appointments, she rarely attended AIDS presentations so missed out on information about how to protect herself from infection. In the years following her first paid sexual encounter, Ouli conceived four more children and contracted HIV. She did not learn her HIV status until a year after Semba was born. Tests later revealed that Semba was HIV negative.

When Ouli's mother returned from Dakar, she made it clear she wanted nothing to do with the children of her "crazy prostitute daughter." She promptly sent Semba to the clinic social worker, who notified Ouli to pick him up. The staff found this ironic because they believed Ouli became crazy and turned to prostitution due to her mother's verbal and physical abuse. Ouli said she was crazy and a prostitute because someone had gone to the *marabout* to put a spell on her. Jealous people often did this, she said. Weeks after she took Semba back, other prostitutes must have been extremely jealous because she was drinking excessively and spending her earnings carelessly. Again, she lost all of Semba's clothes and most of hers.

When I gave Semba some clothes donated by a friend at the embassy, Ouli said they were so nice that she would save them until he could walk. The clinic doctor convinced her that he needed them now and would outgrow them soon. We put an outfit on him and he struggled at first from the restriction. Eventually, he settled into his blue tee shirt and jeans, laughing at his image in the mirror above the sink. Touched by his excitement, Ouli asked me to take a picture of him. I pulled out my camera and photographed both of them.

Soon thereafter, Ouli showed up at the head nurse's house, claiming once again that she could not keep Semba. Again, the head nurse took him for the weekend. During the following week the social worker arranged for an orphanage to take Semba. But when the day came to give him up, Ouli changed her mind. The social worker assured Ouli she could visit Semba at any time, and took him out of her arms. Several months later the social worker said Semba was doing very well at the orphanage and that Ouli was pregnant again despite illnesses associated with AIDS and alcohol abuse.

RUNNING FROM HOME

ROCKHAYA

Unlike Ouli, Rockhaya came from a family that tried to "save" her from prostitution. A tall woman with short fluffy hair and reddish bleached skin, her family held on to her as she tried to sever their relationship. They begged her to stop working, but she proved time and again that she would not. Finally, to appease her father, she said she would go to Mauritania to buy and sell cloth and perfume. She thought she could continue practicing in secret in another country. However, when her father visited to tell her his brother died, he found her among the prostitutes. Khady was with her, and together they talked to Rockhaya's father. At Khady's urging, Rockhaya promised she would return home, though she had no intention of doing so. She would have stayed in Mauritania permanently but, following the evacuation in 1989, she had nowhere to go but home.

Rockhaya visited her family in Dakar on her way to Kaolack, saying she would start a business there. The day she arrived in Kaolack she rented a work hut in Ndangane and was reunited with friends she had made in Mauritania. Months later, her father found her and tried to persuade her to return home, promising to support her. Khady mediated between father and daughter for a second time. Rockhaya promised to leave after receiving her share of the communal kitty Rhama managed. Her turn to receive the money came and went, but still she stayed in Ndangane. She simply could not see herself living at home again, where she would have to share her income and follow her parents' rules.

Like Astou and Nafy, Rockhaya literally ran away from offers of financial support. These women saw moving home as an agreement to surrender their independence and admit defeat in the business world. In the words of the clinic doctor, "prostitutes have more freedom and power than any other Senegalese women." This is true in that prostitution allowed them the independence to earn their own money, decreasing their financial and emotional dependence on sons, fathers, husbands, and boyfriends. While most of the prostitutes said the absence of support from men was the reason they turned to prostitution, these women claimed they stayed in the profession to avoid such dependence. In stark contrast to Khady and Rhama, they would not leave prostitution for a man or for a "more respectable" but lower paying job.

MAGUETTE

Clinic staff and other non-prostitutes interpreted these prostitutes' actions as rebellion against their families and society. In
fact, a few prostitutes, such as Maguette, actually said rebellion was their reason for becoming prostitutes. A hard-looking
thirty-year-old who grew up in Kaolack, Maguette became a
prostitute by associating with "bad company." Her friends
were successful prostitutes who dressed well and resented
their overbearing parents. Angry at her parents for taking
her out of school so she could raise her younger siblings,
Maguette registered at the clinic. She later introduced her
younger sister to the world of prostitution. The sisters lived at
home, sneaking out every night to find clients. And though
they claimed to be rebelling against their families, they took
precautions to protect themselves from HIV, sharing boxes of
condoms they bought at the local pharmacy.

RUNNING FROM THE LAW

Maguette said clandestine prostitutes typically did not register
at the clinic to avoid detection by their families. When they were
ill, they did not go to the STD clinic unless they were desperate,
and even then would never admit to being prostitutes. The
clinic social worker defined a clandestine prostitute as "someone who takes part in prostitution secretly without adhering to
the regulations. She does not want to go to that extreme." In
this way, such women were running from the police and from
the truth that their work was defined as prostitution. Because
Senegalese men often give women gifts and money in exchange
for sex, the line between typical male-female relations and actual prostitution can be fuzzy. But having sex with strangers in
exchange for money, according to the authorities, is definitely
prostitution and it is illegal if the woman is not registered.

Because of failure to register, clandestine prostitutes did not receive free condoms or information about AIDS. Consequently, they rarely required their partners to wear condoms. The police and bar owners estimated that as many as eighty percent of the prostitutes in Kaolack were clandestine (Diop 1987). The clinic doctor estimated that there were ten clandestine prostitutes for every registered one. All agreed the number was rising because the police departments' *brigade des moeurs* (morals brigade) could not afford the gasoline and personnel necessary to search for women without registration cards.

Whereas registered prostitutes worried their families would learn they were registered, clandestine prostitutes feared arrest because they were not registered. Said Amy, whose family knew she registered, "Clandos (clandestine prostitutes) are always afraid and I'm afraid of nothing. I'm regulated." Still, according to the clinic social worker, registered prostitutes who did not tell their families of their work were forced to find creative ways to hide their involvement. Due to constant stress, he said, these women were "always rebelling, always under pressure inside." He added that being a prostitute is humbling, but registering is humiliating. "It's like signing up to be marginalized."

Whereas registered prostitutes admitted their involvement in writing, clandestine prostitutes knew others' suspicion of their involvement could never be validated. There were other differences as well. When clandestine prostitutes married or found other work, they simply stopped practicing. When registered prostitutes decided to stop working, they had to go through a long process before the clinic and police would take them off their rosters. Even when requests were approved and registration relinquished, the clinic kept the women's files. Despite many requests, the social worker continually declined to destroy the evidence, saying he was required to keep the records. Besides, he said, the women would probably re-register when they failed at other economic activities or lost the support of a boyfriend or husband. To save paper, each prostitute registration form had room for three separate registration dates.

The women's fear of detection and life-long stigmatization led several of them to request that their files be destroyed. One woman registered just months before her wedding. The social worker tried to discourage her, but she was determined to earn money as a prostitute and wanted to do it legally. Shortly before her marriage she gave the clinic her withdrawal letter and underwent the required STD tests. She asked for her file but was turned down. A year later, a friend of her husband came across her records at the police department where he worked. He immediately told her husband, who did not wait to hear her explanation before leaving home with their newborn son. The policeman told her to go to the clinic for proof that she stopped practicing before marriage to show her husband. The clinic social worker wrote such a letter, but her husband still refused to let her to see her baby.

Another woman became upset when the social worker would not destroy her file after she stopped practicing. Despite his insistence that no one but clinic staff had access to it, she continued to worry and plead with him. One morning, he found his office broken into and her file gone.

Registered prostitutes and clinic staff said clients usually preferred registered prostitutes over clandestine ones because the former were generally healthier due to regular visits to the clinic and access to free condoms. However, when clandestine prostitutes charged less than registered prostitutes to undercut competition, clients often opted for the lower price.

The behavior of clandestine prostitutes angered registered prostitutes, who showed greater restraint by setting a minimum payment and refusing money from clients who would not wear condoms. Often, such clients would offer up to ten times the normal payment to convince a woman to have unprotected intercourse. Reasoning that one unprotected encounter could eventually make them ill and unable to support their families, most registered prostitutes refused. Clandestine prostitutes, on the other hand, often accepted unprotected sex because they "can't afford to be picky," according to Amy. "Clandos are the ones who get sick, destroy their insides, and sometimes can't have children," added Ndieme.

AWA

Awa, like Maguette, began practicing prostitution to rebel against her wealthy parents. Different from the Ndangane prostitutes who said they tried other economic options and had no choice other than prostitution, Awa maintained she preferred it. She was forty years old, dressed impeccably, and had reached a point in her career where she restricted her clientele to regulars, "not just any man on the street." Instead of paying for a room, she took clients to her room in Anna's house, a large, multi-room building that served as a brothel. Anna, a well-known city councilperson lived elsewhere, but she managed the popular house and its adjoining bar. According to Awa, the women and clients at Anna's were upper-class, far above the "peasants" in Ndangane. When I visited her one evening and asked her how business was, her silence was a sign that my question was inappropriate. In a classy place one does not talk openly about business; in Ndangane, one yells unabashedly from hut to hut broadcasting clients' activities.

It was common knowledge that women who worked in town earned more than ten times the amount Ndangane women earned. Khady accepted the discrepancy, maintaining that the cost of cabfare into town and the mental burden of dealing with drunkards and thieves was not worth the trouble. Other Ndangane prostitutes like Astou were not content with their meager earnings and grew angry at their disrespectful clients, often cheating them out of their money.

DYENEBA

Dyeneba, a Ndangane prostitute for twenty years, took advantage of a client one night by denying that he had given her money for safe keeping while they had intercourse. By his account, he had just received a large amount of cash for his crops and asked her to put his money under the bed. As he dressed in the dark, Dyeneba hid the money in her *pagne*. When he asked for it, she looked under the bed then announced it was gone. Certain that only Dyeneba could have taken it, the client called out for someone to get the police. According to Khady, Dyeneba snuck home and gave her fiance some of the money. She returned to find her work hut full of police. They searched her and, when they found some money tucked in her bra, arrested her. They then tracked down her fiance and arrested him.

I asked Khady what had happened since Dyeneba's arrest. She said that Dyeneba and her fiance remained in prison two months later and continued to deny their guilt. I offered to take her to visit Dyeneba and she accepted eagerly. The next morning I put an orange and a pack of gum into my canvas bag and picked up Khady, who showed me the way to the prison. I parked the car in the shade of the only tree in sight and we walked to the front gate. The guard looked surprised to see a *toubab* until Khady explained that I was the doctor—well, I was on my way to earning a doctorate—of one of their prisoners. The guard said that it was not visiting hours, but went to ask if we could make a short visit. As we walked toward the car to sit in the shade, Khady stopped to speak with an elderly woman balancing a bowl of food on her head. The woman was waiting to visit her son, who was sentenced to prison for several more years. Khady joined me in the car, saying that it is selfish of such criminals to drain their families of money and food. Not only had this deprived his family of potential income, he expected his mother to bring him food each day because the prison diet was inadequate. "Prison is harder on those outside than on those inside," Khady concluded.

A guard approached us and announced that we could go in. He stressed that in the future we could visit only at the designated time. When I asked how many women were in the prison, he said there were three, and that they had rooms separate from the men's. We walked through the gate and were greeted by several more guards, who seemed surprised to see me. Khady and I stood in a small dirt courtyard near several dirty white adobe buildings. The whole compound was surrounded by a chain-link fence.

Led by a guard, Dyeneba walked toward us, squinting from the sunlight. The guard was not armed and let her walk freely. He left her with us and joined the other guards who watched from the shade. Khady introduced me to the plain, middle-aged woman and explained who I was. Dyeneba looked at me and said "I didn't do it, you know." Khady and I said nothing, wondering how she could continue to deny guilt in the face of such strong evidence. Dyeneba said that the man accusing her filed a complaint against her and her fiance, but did not show up on the day of the court hearing. Without him there, the judge would not hear the case and ordered the couple to remain in jail until the accuser went to court. Dyeneba's daughter tried unsuccessfully to convince the judge to change his mind.

Khady told Dyeneba we would do what we could to get her released. I took the orange and gum out of my bag, glancing at the guards to see if they would let me give them to her. When they did not react I handed her them. "I guess they realize these are too small to conceal a weapon or file," I thought, feeling like a character in a crime film. Khady took the pack of gum from Dyeneba, pulled out a piece for herself, then handed it back. It reminded me that inmates were not the only people in Senegal who did not have easy access to luxuries such as chewing gum.

We said goodbye to Dyeneba and the guards then walked through the gate to the car. On our way to Ndangane we dropped by Ibra's office. He said that we should not do anything to help Dyeneba. "She stole money and should be

punished. Do not interfere with the justice system." I agreed
that at least I should leave the case alone, wondering again how
one is supposed to determine how deeply to get involved, if at
all. A week later Khady told me Dyeneba and her husband were
released. She did not know the reason, but she suspected our
visit had something to do with it.

Back in her work hut, Dyeneba showed no remorse for her
crime, and continued stealing from clients when she could.
Many of them made a scene, but she flatly denied her guilt
and managed to avoid arrest. "She's running away from herself and from reality," Khady observed. "Maybe she thinks the
money she steals will help her leave prostitution, but she's
wearing out God's capacity to forgive. Stealing is much worse
than prostitution."

THE GREAT ESCAPE

After hearing of many futile attempts to escape the proverbial
hole that is prostitution, I asked prostitutes and staff for stories about women who had successfully left the profession.
The stories were few. Ndiambe succeeded, in that she stopped
working when she became engaged to Anna's brother. Because she lived in Anna's brothel while waiting for marriage,
Ndiambe kept her registration up to date in case the police
invaded the place. She was one of the lucky ones; her fiance
knew of her work and did not seem bothered by it. Her plan
was to marry him then move away for good.

I heard of another half-dozen women who told their friends
they were leaving prostitution completely. One became a
maid. Another, whose late sister had also been a prostitute,
started a business with money given her by her niece when
her niece received a large bride price from her fiance. Others
left prostitution when their daughters or other female relatives

insisted on it, sometimes physically dragging them out of the clinic. Most who left were not heard from again, so it is impossible to know how they fared.

Most of the prostitutes with young children planned to stop their work before the children were old enough to figure out what their mothers did for a living. This had also been the intention of prostitutes who are now grandmothers. Still, although the dream was rarely realized, it was frequently on their minds. Khady, for example, had a hope chest of sorts. Every week she added dishes and cooking utensils to it, getting further and further into debt to the vendors who passed through the neighborhood. She reasoned that she would need these things when she left Ndangane to start her own household, but failed to acknowledge that her growing debt only delayed her departure. Occasionally, she paid vendors by having sex with them. More often, she hid behind a row of huts when she saw them coming.

RUNNING FROM NDANGANE

Other women in Ndangane revealed that their way of escaping the reality of their work was to take short trips whenever possible. They often followed vendors to weekly markets (*louma*), held in various towns a bus-ride away, where they could find clients among the men from nearby villages. Many of the younger women migrated with the seasons, often defined by annual holidays. In this way, they went home to their families to celebrate the holiday of Tabaski, two months and ten days after Korite, the holiday marking the end of Ramadan. Some of the women would then go to Joal, a fishing village sixty miles south of Dakar, in June or July. In Joal, the main clients were fishermen who migrated south to man fishing boats. Since only boat captains could bring their wives, business was good for the prostitutes. In Joal they earned more per client than they did elsewhere in Senegal and appreciated the convenience of using rented work huts for work and sleep.

When the rainy season ended in October or November, these women traveled east to Mbacke, a small town outside Touba. There they prepared for the arrival of the millions making the pilgrimage. When festivities ended in Touba, the women traveled to Kaolack in time for the pilgrimage commemorating the national holiday, *Gamou* (pilgrimage). During *Gamou*, Kaolack and other large cities were the destination of thousands of pilgrims celebrating the birth of Mohammed. Prostitutes not based in Kaolack often traveled there for clients. Some of them would rent huts in Ndangane for the week. In fact, many Ndangane prostitutes settled in Ndangane after traveling there for the holiday and deciding to stay. Then Ramadan would come around again. For this holiday, prostitutes still close to their families went home to celebrate.

RUNNING ACROSS THE BORDER

Other women not content to stay in Kaolack year-round traveled across the border to the Gambia. They said they preferred the English-speaking country to Senegal for many of the reasons they enjoyed Mauritania. They could buy duty-free goods such as cloth, *boubous*, and perfume, which they sold across the border in Senegal. Although prostitution was illegal in the Gambia, the women were less threatened by the police, who spent little time monitoring the prostitutes. Instead, the police staged annual unannounced round-ups to arrest and transport as many Senegalese prostitutes to the Senegalese police as they could. The women were released quickly and were back in the Gambia within days.

The prostitutes liked the Gambia the most, they said, for a health care system more organized and accommodating than those in Senegal and Mauritania. Gambian health care workers regularly distributed free condoms in the women's places of work and encouraged them to visit the hospital for free medical treatment. The prostitutes also received AIDS education through the clinics.

NDEYE AMY

One of the women who frequented the Gambia was Ndeye Amy, a small, peppy twenty-year-old. An only child, Ndeye Amy grew up in Kaolack and attended school for twelve years to earn a degree as a typist. Unable to find work despite her education, she started work as a prostitute to support her aging parents. She first went to the Gambia to avoid detection by her family and eventually learned that she could make more money there, not only from clients, but also by buying duty-free merchandise to sell elsewhere. To avoid arrest during her visits to Kaolack, she registered at the STD clinic. She did not fear arrest in the Gambia because she had a boyfriend who worked for the police. This liaison proved useful on many occasions, especially when Senegalese prostitutes were expelled from the country after one of them insulted a police officer; Ndeye Amy's boyfriend pulled some strings so she could stay.

This and other forms of migration affected HIV transmission in a variety of ways. In theory, the prostitutes could report to any STD clinic for semimonthly examinations, condoms, and treatment for STDs. In reality, towns and villages they visited often did not have a clinic or other source of condoms. And when there were clinics, they refused to go because they might be recognized. Even on the infrequent occasion that condoms were available in remote villages, their high cost could be prohibitive. Worse, such condoms could not be assumed to be safe due to their age and improper storage conditions.

Despite the physical and social barriers, the women proved they were willing to spend their own money on condoms and to forego money from clients who refused to wear them. While responsible, realistic women like Rhama and Khady were the largest proponents of condom use, "run-away" women demonstrated an amazing ability to control the one part of their lives that demanded premeditation and monetary sacrifice by stocking up on supplies before traveling and turning away non-compliant clients. Despite the excessive drinking and violent actions of the drinkers, their lower rate of STD infection indicates they were heeding the advice of clinic staff and prostitute colleagues by making critical decisions to protect themselves from HIV.

Thus, while many of the women ran away from circumstances and environments that were not desirable, they usually remained true to themselves in their sexual relations with their clients. Still, they occasionally ran from the prostitute community to earn more money and to feel like human beings rather than prostitutes. For similar reasons, some women drank to escape their pain and others stole in hope of buying their way out of it. And others accepted their destiny to remain prostitutes and found the need to run away from their former lives to protect their families and their independence, even when independence meant trading sex for money and living far from their parents and children, who loved and missed them.

In the same manner, the Peace Corps volunteers chose to run away from conditions they found too painful to bear. Like the women who drank or traveled frequently to escape the reality of the situation, the volunteers left their villages in an effort to abandon the circumstances that troubled them. Unlike the prostitutes, however, their livelihood did not depend on their remaining in Senegal. They had traveled to Senegal voluntarily and knew they could travel home voluntarily, putting their troubles behind them.

I saw my situation as falling between those of the volunteers and the women. Like the former, I knew I would soon be traveling home and distancing myself from the circumstances that I found hard to accept. Yet because I understood the women's lives and the various aspects of their culture and society that affected their health, economics, and points of view, I did not want to abandon them. Instead, I wanted to take that knowledge with me and use it in some way to shed light on their plight and their determination to make the best of it. They weren't just running away from some things, it seemed; they were also running toward something, whether it be a more peaceful life or a way to make peace with their current one.

7

Conclusions

... Prostitutes are not problems. They are people. Prostitution is an ancient and very well-established occupation. It is fostered by a huge demand and a multiplicity of social, psychological and economic factors.

(Plant 1990:203)

After completing my interviews, I stayed in Kaolack for two weeks to begin analyzing my data and to ask the prostitutes a few final questions before I moved to Dakar to write my dissertation. I spent most of my days in Ndangane balanced on a backless wooden chair whose uneven legs rocked me in the dirt when I moved. I sat with the women who were not with clients, ending discussions abruptly when an interested man appeared and waited to be noticed. Occasionally, Khady asked if I wanted to watch her with a client, but I declined. Hearing her offer, one man asked who the *toubab* was. "*Toubab*? No. She's my friend," she said as she closed her door.

Two days before I left for Dakar, Rhama and I were talking about condom shortages and how to ensure prostitutes had a constant supply. She had just walked more than a mile from a family planning clinic, where she bought a box of one hundred condoms. Within minutes she emptied the box for her friends, half teasing that they better pay her back soon.

As we talked, a slight, unkempt man appeared from behind the latrine and shyly leaned against Rhama's hut, watching us. Judging from his dress and demeanor, he was a farmer passing through town.

"Four hundred francs," she said, without greeting him.

"Three hundred."

"No. Four." He turned to walk away but Rhama called him back.

"O.K. Three."

Three hundred francs was the minimum amount she would accept from a client. She smiled at me apologetically and slowly lifted her heavy body from the upside-down bucket she used as a stool. She motioned the man into her hut, speaking to him in a lowered voice. Before the cloth in the doorway stopped swaying the couple was back outside. Not in the mood for a confrontation, Rhama pointed to me. "See that *toubab*? She's here to make sure you wear a condom." The man looked at me as if he had not seen me earlier. He nodded and disappeared into the hut. Rhama winked and closed the metal door behind her.

For an instant I felt self-important, as if I had really played a role in AIDS prevention in a high-risk population. Then I realized I was a mechanism. I appreciated that Rhama acknowledged my efforts, but I knew that I was one of many reasons she has used in her successful efforts to convince clients to wear condoms. Some days, she yells to her friends to back her up; some days she says that an authority figure, such as the clinic doctor or a *marabout*, will get angry if she forgoes use; some days she simply gives the reluctant man his money back and tells him to go away so she can finish her conversation with her friends.

Moments after Rhama and her client closed her hut door, Astou joined me in the shade, sitting on the sunken bucket. I offered her my chair, but she refused. Then she suggested we share it, so we both sat on the narrow wooden seat, putting our arms around each other to stay on. She said she was sad I was leaving and asked me to bring her a *toubab* dress to remember me by. The next day I gave her my largest dress, dark green with small yellow and red flowers, in hope that its loose skirt would fit around her large hips. She thanked me, clasping her hands together as if in prayer, then broke into a song and dance.

On my last visit to Ndangane, Khady greeted me enthusiastically as I got out of my car. She was laughing and almost running across the compound, her *boubou* flowing over her bouncing body.

"You should have seen Astou last night!" she raved. Fearing the worst, I asked what happened.

"She put on your dress and some *toubab* shoes and danced for us!"

"Oh," I sighed, sad at the thought of all I would be missing. "I'm sorry I missed it."

"Let's go get her now. She'll put it on for you."

We walked around the corner and up the dirt path to Astou's work hut.

"Astou, your daughter is coming!" yelled one of the palm wine salesmen. No response. We peered in her door and found her asleep. She looked so calm and vulnerable, curled in a fetal position on her thin foam mattress propped on truck tires. No large wig or posturing or crazy antics. I motioned that we should leave, but Khady woke her with a shake of a shoulder and told her to put on her *toubab* outfit. Astou looked bewildered for an instant then perked up and started to change her clothes. We went back to our seats to wait.

After a few minutes Astou came around the corner. The dress was quite snug at the hips and her black wig resembled a bouffant hairdo. On her feet were open-toed platform shoes like those worn with bell bottoms in the 1970's. She walked toward us provocatively, swinging her hips from left to right, her hands and arms in rhythm. After a few steps she stopped and struck a pose with one hand on her hip and the other on her wig as she batted her eyelashes. We laughed hard, the sort that makes problems fade.

When she reached us, Astou began to sing and dance. Women on the other side of the huts heard her and rounded the corner. They formed a circle around her, clapping and cheering her on as she strutted, shook her rear end, and tilted her head suggestively. Her arthritic ankle was swollen, but there was no hint of a limp.

"You are not like a cigarette," she sang to me. "You have a lot of weight as a person of character, so no one could ever throw you out of a window." The women clapped and called my name.

"Coumba! Coumba!"

"As my rear end follows me," Astou added, "I will follow you."

I was very touched and beckoned her to take my chair. She sat down, legs together, as I stood at her side. The excitement and laughter began to subside. Then, in after thought, she propped her right ankle on her left knee.

"I forgot! I'm a *toubab*!" she exclaimed, pretending to be me. Once again laughter echoed through the weathered thatch huts of Ndangane.

Seeing her in that pose made me realize that I had often forgotten to sit in a culturally-appropriate way, and I smiled at her keen perception. Astou may have been suffering physically and emotionally, but her unfading sense of humor and charm kept all present laughing and clapping, oblivious to the dust and men and problems hovering about. When her audience quieted down, Astou looked me in the eye.

"I wish you a very successful life and two healthy children." The others chimed in.

"Michelle, will you stop by the clinic and tell them Couna isn't feeling well?" Rhama asked. As I said yes, it struck me that, knowing I would be leaving, she had begun calling me by my American name two weeks earlier.

"Don't forget your sisters and mothers," Khady smiled. Saye clasped her breast and added that I should be sure to greet my American mother for my Senegalese mother. As I motioned that it was time to go, some of the women shook my hand and others hugged me.

It was a sweet farewell and the happiest of my times in Ndangane. I told them that I would not forget them and thanked them for their friendship and support. *"Noko bokk,"* they replied. We are all in it together.

The most difficult part of my fieldwork was getting into my car and driving away from Ndangane after Astou's performance. Whereas I once worried that I would be biased against them because of their profession, I was leaving with respect, admiration, and appreciation for people whose stories would have an impact on me long after I left the field. And now when I catch myself sitting with my right ankle on my left knee, I picture the courageous and charismatic Astou in a green *toubab* dress imitating me.

****

Because I was privileged to hear some of the stories of people normally represented only by HIV surveillance statistics, my purpose in this book has been to convey the significance of their daily experiences by describing their decisions and dilemmas amid strong pressure to comply with social roles and cultural expectations. Only through attention to such details can anthropologists and other AIDS researchers come to a true understanding of the factors that facilitate and impede positive behavior change. (See, for example: Caravano 1991; De Bruyn 1992; De Cock et al 1994; Gupta and Weiss 1993; Heise and Elias 1995; Herdt 1991; Kane and Mason 1992; Karim 1995; McGrath et al 1993; Moses 1994; Orubuloye 1993; Schoepf 1992; Taylor 1990; and Ulin 1992). Not surprisingly, the prostitutes' experiences and responses are similar to those of poor and disenfranchised women throughout the world, reminding us that much is to be learned in our efforts to design effective HIV education programs and to facilitate women's attempts to change their own behavior and that of the people who influence them. As Worth (1989:306) has explained,

> The women who are most vulnerable to HIV infection are those who have the least control over their sexual decision making, whether because of drug use, lack of economic power, culturally sanctioned gender-role behavior, racism, or sexism.

Despite differences in life histories, living situations, devotion to Islam, and mechanisms for coping with life as a prostitute, the women chronicled here share the common goal of making a living and preserving their health in spite of societal pressures, economic barriers, and male domination. As the women's stories testify, the issues affecting their lives are not confined to the daily occurrences inside and around the huts in Ndangane, but are manifest in the societal pressures and constraints that limit the freedom and opportunities of all women, not just those who have registered as prostitutes.

In a simplified model of these influences, one might envision a society comprised of three concentric circles: "mainstream" culture, community, and family. The first and largest, mainstream culture represents the overarching beliefs and expectations enforced by Islam on the one hand, and non-religious cultural factors on the other hand. These two systems are so intertwined in Senegal that even the Senegalese have difficulty separating the sacred from the secular. For instance, practices and beliefs that pre-dated Islam in Senegal are often attributed to religion, and Muslim tenets are frequently presented as cultural norms deemed applicable to all Senegalese regardless of religion and ethnic group.

These Islamic and cultural standards of normalcy and morality are reinforced within the second circle, community, and the third circle, family. Individuals are located at the very center of these three circles, and their thoughts and dreams are shaped by their families' and communities' reinforcement of the standards by which they are judged throughout their lives. Little girls and married women learn through observation and the words of religious and other leaders that their role is substantially different from that of boys and men. They are told men will provide for them and are encouraged to learn skills that will complement those of their husbands. Despite recent progress toward achieving greater access to education, training, and income-generating positions, Senegalese women's primary domain remains the household, where they perform domestic tasks and receive an allowance from their working husbands. When such women divorce, their families and communities are expected to provide them a safety net to compensate for the loss of support. When women do not have access to such support they are forced to make a living with little or no education or skills. Most prostitutes said they turned to prostitution as a last resort and, knowing that they no longer met societal and familial expectations, distanced themselves literally and figuratively from their communities and families, once the focus in their lives.

Prostitutes who live with their families and work in town manage to maintain an appearance of conformity by remaining at home and concealing their activities. In contrast, prostitutes who live alone and work in Ndangane may continue to visit their families in other towns and lie about their activities, but their sense of community shifted when they moved away from their families. Once in Kaolack, even though they would never call it home, they begin to rely heavily on the STD clinic for medical care, health information, and occasional shelter from a society that shuns them. More importantly, their sense of value comes not from the people who raised them or from clinic staff who often criticize them, but from the women with whom they live and work. Through time, their relationships take on the structure and function of a family, replete with generations and hierarchies, alliances and communally-solved disputes. Eventually, a life characterized by marriage, daily prayers, and morality seems beyond their reach. It remains a dream and a goal, but the women eventually acknowledge its unlikelihood.

The communal spirit and solidarity of the women in Ndangane has kept them afloat in a sea of criticism and stigma. In the age of AIDS, it has played a vital role in keeping them alive. Even women who were infected prior to receiving AIDS education have benefited in that, well before knowing their own status, they made efforts that protected them from other STDs and prevented transmission to their clients. In many ways it is ironic that participants in a profession demanding independence and competitiveness have joined forces in this manner. In fact, although their first allegiance continues to be to themselves and to the people they support through their work, prostitutes in Ndangane recognize that their individual needs—namely to protect themselves from infection so as to continue earning an income to support themselves and their families—are best met through preservation of the community and widespread agreement about behavioral norms.

In no way is this world view better illustrated than in their dedication to controlling the nature of sexual relations with clients. Knowing that clients will pay more money for unprotected sex and that one woman's failure to enforce safe sex breaks down the communal effort, the women have drastically altered their own behavior and that of their clients. Given the typically unequal nature of male-female relations in Senegal, this represents a successful shift in power and control over sexual behaviors from men to women. It is true that this shift has occurred at a very basic level within a much larger male-dominated society, but it is a concrete example of actions and attitudes that can result from effective AIDS prevention education, which has the potential to bring about cross-cutting behavior and attitudinal change in Senegal and elsewhere. It also speaks to the necessity to assure women equal access to education, economic opportunities, and political power so that they have more options to choose from and more leverage in their relationships with men.

The path to increased control over sexual relations with clients was not an easy one, but its milestones are easy to identify. The necessary elements were the relationships between the women and the dedication of clinic staff to providing the women with appropriate advice for staying healthy and avoiding HIV infection. Even though the relationships between clinic staff and prostitutes were often tense and some of the staff's actions actually impeded the women's efforts to enforce condom use, the prostitutes valued the advice given them and benefited from the accurate and accessible information about transmission. This is due to clinic staff's own contextual analysis, which identified the medical, economic, religious, and social issues most important in the women's lives. These were then incorporated into safe-sex messages that appealed to the prostitutes' need for control over their health and convinced them of the necessity of behavior change. The next step was for the women to educate the men in their lives and to challenge sexual roles.

This proved easier in their dealings with clients than with boyfriends, as it has for prostitutes in a variety of cultural and social contexts (Day 1990; Green et al. 1993; Kane and Mason 1992; Plant 1990; Rosenberg and Weiner 1988). Ndangane prostitutes, for their part, drew on their negotiation skills to enforce condom use once they determined that money lost through turning away non-compliant clients is inconsequential when weighed against the cost of illness. Although the women's reported increase in condom use cannot be directly verified, the clinic staff documented a significant decline in STD rates and HIV seroconversion since the inception of the campaign (Gueye 1992; Lewis 1993). While this could be due to a number of factors, the women credited the clinic with their change in behavior because the clinic educated them about the need for behavior change and required them with condoms, though not always in sufficient amounts. Still, the evidence is clear that their clients wore condoms often enough to make a profound difference. It has been shown that when condoms are used by the majority of people the majority of the time, a campaign is successful and transmission is substantially curtailed (Moses et al. 1993). With lower rates of STDs, resulting ulcers and infections decrease and seroconversion declines, even when condoms are not worn during every sexual encounter.

Still, the women have had less success in their attempts to protect themselves during sex with boyfriends than with clients. This has been found to be the case in other cultures as well (Day 1990; Green et al. 1993; Kane and Mason 1992; Plant 1990; Rosenberg and Weiner 1988; De Zalduondo 1991; De Zalduondo and Hernandez-Avila 1990). Despite some knowledge about AIDS, the boyfriends continue to view women's desire to use condoms as indication that the women may be infected or that the women suspect the men are unfaithful. Because the boyfriends represent a possible way out of prostitution, many women have decided the cost of losing such emotional and financial support is higher than the risk of infection. In this respect, prostitutes are no different from non-prostitutes: both groups of women depend on the support of their sexual partners and are willing to place themselves at risk for HIV infection to maintain their relationships. In this light, labeling prostitutes as a high-risk group is not accurate. Rather, it is in their role as girlfriends and wives that Senegalese women—prostitutes and non-prostitutes alike—face the highest risk of infection because they report little if any condom use. All non-prostitutes in the study contracted an STD at least once in their lives, which is proof of their involvement in unprotected sex with men who could expose them to other STDs, including HIV. Clearly, even women who are well informed about HIV and want to protect themselves have not secured the power required to negotiate the nature of their relations with male partners in and out of the bedroom. In fact, only women like Fatou, who refuse to be involved with men other than compliant clients, will remain safe from infection and conflict until condom use no longer constitutes a compromise. For these reasons, prostitutes, like other women who do not enforce condom use by boyfriends, are at high risk because of this particular behavior, regardless of membership in a group labeled high-risk.

Given the universal constraints, any step toward equality and behavior modification is a significant one. It is unfortunate, however, that these extraordinary women do not recognize their own progress and power nor do they realize that their actions have made a significant difference in their lives and in the lives of those who will follow them to similar crossroads. Still, it is important that the progress made by the women in Ndangane and others like them around the world should be documented, compared, and repeated with attention to social, economic, and political context. True, the statistical evidence amassed by the clinic demonstrates on its own that behavior change has taken place and that lives have been saved through condom use. Yet no matter how impressive the numbers are, it is only through individual voices that we can learn of the milestones and obstacles the women behind the numbers encountered on the path to long-term behavior change and understand how they made informed decisions about where to go at each crossroad. The women in Ndangane have contained the threat of HIV within the realm over which they have control. It is important to remember Khady's words: "I avoid AIDS with all my power." The next step is to draw on the lessons she and others have learned to expand education to, and elicit behavior change from, the powerful people and ideologies comprising the larger circles that surround and affect the lives of people like the women of Ndangane.

References

Agar, Michael H. 1980 The Professional Stranger: An Informal Introduction to Ethnography. Orlando: Academic Press.

Airhihenbuwa, Collins O. 1989 Perspectives on AIDS in Africa: Strategies for Prevention and Control. AIDS Education and Prevention 1(1): 57–69.

Ba, Edwige Bienvenu 1991 Experience de la Mise sur Pied d'Un Programme de Reinsertion et de Reconversion d'Une Population Presentant Un Haut Risque de Contamination à HIV à Kaolack. Dakar: University of Dakar.

Bernard, H. Russell 1988 Research Methods in Cultural Anthropology. Newberry Park, California: Sage Publications.

Bongaarts, John, Priscilla Reining, Peter Way and Francis Conant 1989 The Relation of Male Circumcision to HIV Infection in African Populations. AIDS 3:373–377.

Brooks, George E., Jr. 1976 The Signares of Saint-Louis and Gorée: Women Entrepreneurs in Eighteenth-Century Senegal. In Women in Africa: Studies in Social and Economic Change. Nancy J. Hafkin and Edna Bay, eds. pp 19–44. Stanford: Stanford University Press.

De Bruyn, Maria 1992 Women and AIDS in Developing Countries. Social Science and Medicine 34(3): 249– 262.

Caldwell, John C., I.O. Orubuloye and Pat Caldwell 1992 Underreaction to AIDS in Sub-Saharan Africa. Social Science and Medicine 34(11): 1169–1182.

Caravano, Kathryn 1991 More than Mothers and Whores: Redefining the AIDS Prevention Needs of Women. International Journal of Health Services. 21(1): 131–142.

Carr, Dolores 1985 Senegal. Dakar: United States Embassy.

De Cock, Kevin M., Ehounou Ekpini, Emmanuel Gnaore, Auguste Kadio and Helene Gayle 1994 The Public Health Implications of AIDS Research in Africa. Journal of the American Medical Association. 272(6): 481–486.

Creevey, Lucy 1991 Impact of Islam on Women in Senegal. Journal of Developing Areas. April: 1–32.

Day, Sophie 1990 Prostitution and the Ideology of Work in London. In Culture and AIDS. Douglas Feldman, ed. pp 93–110. NY: Praeger.

Diop, Mbody 1987 Islam et la Prostitution. Le Soleil. November 1, 1987.

Farmer, Paul 1992 AIDS and Accusation: Haiti and the Geography of Blame. Berkeley: University of California Press.

FHI (Family Health International) 1989 Surveillance Obstetrical dans la Region Medicale de Kaolack, Senegal Rapport Final. Dakar: Family Health International.

Forster, Sarah J. and Kemlin E. Furley 1988 Public Awareness Survey on AIDS and Condoms in Uganda. AIDS 3:147–154.

Frake, Charles 1961 The Diagnosis of Disease Among the Subuanum of Mindanao. American Anthropologist 63:113–132.

Gellar, Sheldon 1982 Senegal: An African Nation Between Islam and the West. Boulder: Westview.

Gladwin, Christina 1989 Ethnographic Decision Tree Modeling. Newberry Park: Sage.

Green, S.T., D.J. Goldberg, P.R. Christie, M. Frischer, A. Thomson, S.V. Carr and A. Taylor 1993 Female Streetworker—Prostitutes in Glasgow: A Descriptive Study of Their Lifestyle. AIDS Care 5(3): 321–335.

Gueye, El Hadj 1992 Interviews with the Director of the Centre MST of Kasnack in Kaolack, Senegal.

Global Programme on AIDS 1995 The Current Global Situation of the HIV/AIDS Pandemic. Geneva: World Health Organization.

Gupta, Geeta Rao and Ellen Weiss 1993 Women and AIDS: Developing a New Strategy. International Council for Research on Women.

Heath, Deborah 1988 The Politics of Signifying Practices in Kaolack, Senegal: Hegemony and the Dialectic of Autonomy and Domination. Doctoral Dissertation: Johns Hopkins University.

Heise, Lori L. and Christopher Elias. 1995 Transforming AIDS Prevention to Meet Women's Needs: A Focus on Developing Countries. Social Science and Medicine. 40(7):931–943.

Herdt, Gilbert 1991 AIDS and Anthropology. Anthropology Today 3:1–3.

Ingstad, Benedicte 1990 The Cultural Construction of AIDS and Its Consequences for Prevention in Botswana. Medical Anthropology Quarterly 4(1): 28–40.

Kane, Stephanie and Theresa Mason 1992 "IV Drug Users" and "Sex Partners": The Limits of Epidemiological Categories and the Ethnography of Risk. In The Time of AIDS: Social Analysis, Theory and Method. Gilbert Herdt and Shirley Lindenbaum, eds. pp 199–222. Newberry Park: Sage.

Karim, Quarraisha Abdool, Salim S. Abdool Karim, DipData, Kate Soldan and Martin Zondi 1995 Reducing the Risk of HIV Infection among South African Sex Workers: Socio–economic and Gender Barriers. American Journal of Public Health. 85(11): 1521–1525.

Kleinman, Arthur 1978 Concepts and a Model for the Comparison of Medical Systems as Cultural Systems. Social Science and Medicine 12:85–93.

Kreiss, J.K. and S.G. Hopkins 1993 The Association Between Circumcision Status and Human Immunodeficiency Virus Infection Among Homosexual Men. Journal of Infectious Disease 168(6):1408.

Leap, William 1991 AIDS, Linguistics and the Study of Non-Neutral Discourse. Special Issue: Anthropology, Sexuality and AIDS. The Journal of Sex Research 28(2): 275–288.

Lee, Mary 1989 Etude sur l'Utilisation et l'Acceptabilité des Preservatifs Parmi des Prostituées au Centre du Kasnack à Kaolack. Unpublished.

Lewis, Michelle 1993 AIDS, Gender and Behavior Change: Women's Responses to the Pandemic in Urban Senegal. Doctoral Dissertation: The American University, Washington, D.C.

Little, Kenneth 1973 African Women in Towns: An Aspect of Africa's Social Revolution. London: Cambridge University Press.

Mboup, Souleymane 1992 Interviews with the Director of AIDS Research, Hôpital le Dantec. Dakar, Senegal.

McGrath, Janet W., Charles B. Rwabukwali, Debra A. Schumann, Jonnie Pearson-Marks, Sylvia Nakayiwa, Barbar Namande, Lucy Nakyobe and Rebecca Mukasa 1993 Anthropology and AIDS: The Cultural Context of Sexual Risk Behavior Among Urban Baganda Women in Kampala, Uganda. Social Science and Medicine. 36(4): 429–439.

Messing, Simon 1990 The Problem of "Operations Based on Custom" in Applied Anthropology: The Challenge of the Hosken Report on Genital and Sexual Mutilations of Females. Human Organization 39(3).

Morgan, Robin, ed. 1984 Sisterhood is Global: The International Women's Movement Anthology. Garden City, NY: Anchor Press/Doubleday.

Moses, Stephen, Francis A. Plummer, Elizabeth N. Ngugi and Nico J. Nakelkerke 1993 Controlling HIV in Africa: Effectiveness and Cost of an Intervention in a High-Frequency STD Transmitter Core Group. AIDS 5(4): 407–411.

Ndiaye, Salif, Ibrahima Sarr and Mohamed Ayad 1986 Enquête Demographique et de Santé au Senegal. Columbia, MD: Institute for Resource Development/Westinghouse.

Nelson, Harold D. 1974 Area Handbook for Senegal. Washington, DC: Library of Congress.

Pillsbury, Barbara 1990 Sociocultural Factors Influencing the Delivery and Use of Health and Family Planning Services in Senegal. Senegal: USAID.

Plant, Martin 1990 Conclusions and Future Strategies. In AIDS, Drugs and Prostitutes. Martin Plant, ed. London: Routledge.

Rabinow, Paul 1977 Reflections of Fieldwork in Morocco. Berkeley: University of California Press.

Renaud, Michelle Lewis 1993 "We're All in It Together": AIDS Prevention in Urban Senegal. Practicing Anthropology 15(4): 25–29.

Rosenberg, Michael J. and Jodie M. Weiner 1988 Prostitutes and AIDS: A Health Department Priority? American Journal of Public Health 78(4):418–423.

Savane, Marie Angelique 1984 Senegalese Women. In Sisterhood is Global: The International Women's Movement Anthology. Robin Morgan, ed. Garden City, NY: Anchor Press/Doubleday.

Schoepf, Brooke Grundfest 1992 Women at Risk: Case Studies from Zaire. In The Time of AIDS: Social Analysis, Theory and Method. Gilbert Herdt and Shirley Lindenbaum, eds. pp 259–286. Newberry Park: Sage.

Spradley, James P. 1972 Adaptive Strategies of Urban Nomads: The Ethnoscience of Tramp Culture. In The Anthropology of Urban Environments.

Thomas Weaver and Douglas White, eds. pp 21–38. Boulder: Society for Applied Anthropology.

Taylor, Christopher C. 1990 Condoms and Cosmology: The 'Fractal' Person and Sexual Risk in Rwanda. Social Science and Medicine. 31(9): 1023–1028.

Ulin, Priscilla R. 1992 African Women and AIDS: Negotiating Behavior Change. Social Science and Medicine. 34(1): 63–73.

Van de Walle, Etienne 1990 The Social Impact of AIDS in Sub-Saharan Africa. The Milbank Quarterly 68(1):10–32.

Viadro, Claire 1991 Identification des Obstacles a un Counseling Efficace des Patients VIH Seropositifs et de Leur Entourage au Senegal: Cas de la Clinique des Maladies Infectieuses. Dakar: Population Council.

Worth, Dooley 1989 Sexual Decision-Making and AIDS: Why Condom Promotion Among Vulnerable Women is Likely to Fail. Studies in Family Planning 20(6):297–306.

Yoder, P. Stanley 1980 Issues in the Study of Ethnomedical Systems in Africa. In African Health and Healing Systems: Proceedings of a Symposium. P. Stanley Yoder, ed. pp 1–20. Los Angeles: Crossroads Press.

De Zalduondo, Barbara O. 1991 Prostitution Viewed Cross-Culturally: Toward Recontextualizing Sex Work in AIDS Intervention Research. Special Issue: Anthropology, Sexuality and AIDS. Journal of Sex Research 28(2): 223–248.

De Zalduondo, B. and M. Hernandez-Avila 1990 Intervention strategies for reducing HIV transmission among female commercial sex workers and their clients. In AIDS and Reproductive Health. J. Sepulveda, S. Segal and L. Chen, eds. Proceedings from the Conference on AIDS and Reproductive Health, Oct. 1–5, 1990.